The Ch
GREAT

The Christian's
GREAT ENEMY

*A Practical Exposition
of 1 Peter 5:8–11*

John Brown

*Be sober, be vigilant; because your adversary the devil, as a
roaring lion, walketh about, seeking whom he may devour:
whom resist steadfast in the faith . . .*
1 PETER 5:8–11.

THE BANNER OF TRUTH TRUST

THE BANNER OF TRUTH TRUST

3 Murrayfield Road, Edinburgh EH12 6EL, UK
P.O. Box 621, Carlisle, PA 17013, USA

*

First published in *Expository Discourses on 1 Peter*
(1848) and reprinted in *1 Peter, vol. 2* by the
Banner of Truth Trust, 1975

This edition first published 2013
© The Banner of Truth Trust 2013

ISBN:
Print: 978 1 84871 308 6
EPUB: 978 1 84871 365 9
Kindle: 978 1 84871 366 6

*

Typeset in 11/14 pt Sabon Oldstyle Figures
at the Banner of Truth Trust, Edinburgh

Printed in the USA by
Versa Press, Inc.,
East Peoria, IL

CONTENTS

FOREWORD

Christians often speak about 'the person and work of Christ'—who he is and what he has done for us. But the Bible itself never thinks about the Lord Jesus in merely abstract terms and categories. It portrays him as coming into the decisive point of a true story whose plot line goes backwards to the creation of the world and the events of the Garden of Eden, and then forwards to the consummation of all things and the restoration of Eden in the new heavens and earth.

This story can be viewed from several different perspectives. It begins with the Fall. It leads to the Incarnation and to all that Christ accomplished through his death and resurrection, undoing what took place at the Fall. His sacrificial death effected expiation (the cleansing of our guilt), propitiation (of God's wrath), justification (instead of our condemnation), and reconciliation (instead of our alienation).

But in fact the Bible's earliest perspective on the work of Christ focuses our attention elsewhere—although it implies all of these dimensions. For the first promise of salvation in Genesis 3:15 (what earlier Christians called the *Protevangelion*—the first gospel announcement), is, in effect, a promise of ongoing conflict leading to final victory. The seed of the serpent and the seed of the woman (Eve) will stand in opposition to each other throughout history. One day one particular seed of the woman will engage in a climactic and bloody battle with the serpent. The serpent's head will be crushed by the woman's seed whose own heel will be crushed in the process. The rest of the Bible is, in essence, the outworking of this gospel prophecy.

We often lose sight of this (it is a tactic of the serpent of course). While we rejoice in the forgiveness of our sins, and the end of sin's reign over us through the death and resurrection of Christ, we forget the fact that we have an enemy. Yes, he has been defeated (Christ triumphed over him at the cross, *Col.* 2:15); but he has not yet been finally banished to the lake of fire (*Rev.* 20:10). So, just as we daily battle against sin (its guilt is forgiven, its reign is ended, but its presence is an ongoing reality in our lives against which we struggle daily), so too, according to the Apostle Peter, we must be constantly on guard against the schemes of the devil (*1 Pet.* 5:8-9; *cf. 2 Cor.* 2:11). While Paul says that we are not ignorant of them, the sad truth is we often seem to be. Only the armour of God is adequate defence. But we need instruction on when and how to wear it. And in the nature of the case (since our enemy is a deceiver) we need to be constantly reminded of this.

This, above all, is why the republication of John Brown's brief and readable study of 'The Christian's Great Enemy' is both timely and helpful. For younger Christians it will provide a pocket manual for spiritual warfare. At the same time it will serve as a refresher course for more seasoned Christians who are aware of their own weakness and forgetfulness.

All of us need regular spiritual recalibration. John Brown provides us with an important checkup directory. Unlike many contemporary modern books, this one is free from anecdotes. Nor do John and Jane, Simon and Sarah make an appearance in Dr Brown's office only to have their problems resolved by his counselling (as is the genre of much writing today). John Brown himself is never the hero in these pages. No, here there is only the solid counsel of careful biblical exposition, biblical illustration, and biblical application from a man with unusual intellectual skills (he was professor to his denomination's students for the ministry), widely-appreciated pastoral gifts (some 1,600 people crowded to hear his expository preaching), and enormous spiritual maturity (these pages come from the seventh decade of his life). But this—careful biblical instruction, wise pastoral application, seasoned personal devotion to Christ—is in fact what we really need, especially when it comes with the kind of spiritual illumination that sheds light on our situation and circumstances and helps us to see things more clearly.

Here, then, Dr Brown encourages us with the simple, yet perspective-transforming and resistance-strengthening thought that 'the Christian who is enabled to triumph over temptation, is stronger than if he had never been tempted.' Here too, we are reminded that Satan's influence is 'very powerful, though not physically irresistible.' John Brown allows neither pessimism nor determinism to permeate our Christian thinking.

John Brown (1784–1858)

John Brown came from one of the most distinguished family lines in the history of Scottish ministers. Both his father and his (more famous) grandfather (both 'John') had been ministers before him in the Secession Church which owed its origins to the breach in the Church of Scotland precipitated by Ebenezer Erskine and others in the previous (eighteenth) century. Born in Whitburn in 1784, he was licensed as a preacher in 1805 (he apparently preached 'dressed in light coloured knee breeches and hessian boots'!). Thereafter he served successively in Biggar (1806–22), Rose Street, Edinburgh (1822–29), and finally in Broughton Place, Edinburgh (1829–58), where he remained until his death. Extraordinarily widely read, and hugely respected as a Christian leader, he was first and foremost a pastor to his people, sharing their joys and sorrows, triumphs and failures—as they also shared his. His first wife, Jane, died after only nine years of marriage. Nineteen years later he married again, only to lose his second wife, Margaret, some six years later, and his five year old daughter a few years afterwards. He knew intimately the trials of the Christian believer and the points at which Satan malevolently attacks him.

Brown's ministry was characterised by his faithfulness to Scripture. One of the features that marks all his work is his attention to the flow and inner logic of Scripture. He laboured diligently to lay bare the meaning of a passage and then to build his exposition and application on that. For that reason there is a deceptive simplicity coupled with a wonderful clarity in everything he writes.

His preaching expounded the text, rather than use it as a starting point for a thematic discourse. In the pulpit he would frequently comment on some interpretation or application of his text: 'This is truth, important truth and truth taught elsewhere in Scripture, but not the truth contained in this passage.' He kept his people's minds fixed on Scripture itself and sought to anchor his applications from within the text itself. It was well said about Brown's handling of biblical truth that he had 'a way of getting at the kernel without breaking your teeth upon the shell'! The result was, as his colleague and successor commented during his funeral sermon, 'You knew your Bible better when you left the church than when you entered it.' It is impossible to read this particular sample of his expository powers without feeling exactly that.

The Christian's Great Enemy

The Christian's Great Enemy is in fact only an extract from Brown's monumental *Expository Discourses on 1 Peter*. First published in three volumes in 1848 it illustrates the ripest fruit of his long ministry. He had expounded 1 Peter both in the context of his pulpit ministry and also in his classroom lectures to theological students. Thus the mature expression of his studies here is rooted in a lifetime of meditation on the text. It will be enjoyed best, and be most helpful, if it is read at leisure rather than devoured at speed. And the 'taste' of its teaching will improve on a second helping!

John Brown's handling of 1 Peter 5:8-11 is simplicity and lucidity itself, but perhaps a glance at his 'road map' will provide some orientation at the beginning of the journey. His route through the text is as follows:

Introduction

I. The Christian's Great Enemy

(1.) Who is he? The Devil
(2.) What is he?
    (i.) He is a real adversary

(ii.) He is a subtle adversary

(iii.) He is an active adversary

(iv.) He is a cruel adversary

(v.) He is a powerful adversary

II. The Christian's Duty in Reference to his Great Enemy

(1.) What he must do—resist him

(i.) Resist his attacks on himself

(ii.) Resist his attacks on the Christian cause

(2.) What he must do in order to resist him

(i.) He must be sober

(ii.) He must be vigilant

(iii.) He must be steadfast

III. The Christian's Encouragements to Perform his Duty in Reference to his Enemy

(1.) The encouraging fact—all Christians sustain this struggle

(2.) (i) The encouragement contained in the promise

(a.) They shall be made perfect

(b.) They shall be established

(c.) They shall be strengthened

(d.) They shall be settled

(e) The one who does this for us is God himself

(ii.) The encouragement in the appendages to this promise

(a.) The promising God is the God of all grace

(b.) This grace called us 'in Christ Jesus.'

(c.) This God called us to his eternal glory

       (d.) Our afflictions are moderate, short, and
            part of God's plan

IV. Conclusion

Now, read on, travel slowly, and become better
prepared for the fight!

SINCLAIR B. FERGUSON
Dundee
9 October, 2013

INTRODUCTION[1]

Be sober, be vigilant; because your adversary the devil, as a roaring lion, walketh about, seeking whom he may devour; whom resist stedfast in the faith, knowing that the same afflictions are accomplished in your brethren that are in the world. But the God of all grace, who hath called us unto his eternal glory by Christ Jesus, after that ye have suffered a little while, make you perfect, stablish, strengthen, settle you: to him be glory and dominion forever and ever. Amen. — 1 Pet. 5:8-11.

There is, perhaps, no article of revealed truth which has been more generally ridiculed by infidels, and probably, for that reason more frequently attempted to be explained away by philosophizing Christians, than the doctrine of the existence and agency of evil spirits. That among professed Christians highly absurd notions on this subject have been entertained, and to a certain extent, are still

---

[1] Discourse 23 in John Brown, *1 Peter, vol.* 2 (Edinburgh: Banner of Truth, 1975), pp. 556-612.

I

entertained, I am not disposed to question: but surely revelation cannot be fairly charged with the errors and absurdities of those who profess to believe it, unless it can be satisfactorily proved that it gives sanction to these errors and absurdities.

In the present instance it will be no difficult task to show that no such sanction is afforded, and that in the doctrine of the existence and agency of evil spirits, as taught in the Holy Scriptures, there is nothing irrational or ridiculous. For what is their doctrine on this subject? It may be thus briefly stated: 'There exists a numerous race of unembodied intelligent beings, occupying a higher place than man in the general scale of existence, who have lost the moral integrity in which they were created, and who, though under the control of the supreme Providence, are constantly engaged in an attempt, by a variety of methods, and particularly by influencing, in a malignant manner, the minds of men, to uphold and extend the empire of evil in the universe of God.' Now, what principle of reason, what appearance in nature, what well-established fact, what declaration of Scripture, is contradicted by this doctrine? I know of none. Let us look at the subject a little more closely.

That there should be morally imperfect, that is, wicked creatures, in a world which owes its origin and continued existence to an all-perfect Being, infinite in power and wisdom, holiness and benignity; and that a being, capable of moral judgment, and possessed of free agency, should refuse the greatest good, and choose the greatest evil, are mysterious facts, for which no man can fully account, but of which surely no rational man can seriously doubt. Every man has their evidence, alas! but too abundant, around him and within him. Man certainly is a depraved intelligent being; and if it be certain that there are depraved embodied spirits, it would be difficult to prove that there cannot be depraved unembodied spirits.

The mode in which these immaterial agents influence human character, and conduct, and destiny, may safely be acknowledged to be inexplicable; but the fact that they do possess and exert such influence, is not on this ground, if supported by appropriate and adequate evidence, incredible. The mode in which one human mind influences another, though no sane person can doubt of the fact, is involved in equal mystery. It is not more wonderful, nor on sufficient evidence more difficult to be believed, in some points of view it is less so, that one spiritual being should act on another, without the intervention of bodily organs, than that by certain conventional sounds conveyed to the ear, or certain arbitrary characters presented to the eye, the thoughts and feelings of one embodied spirit should be communicated to another embodied spirit, and become the instruments of altering opinion, exciting desire, stimulating to action.

The agency of the evil spirits on the human mind is no more inconsistent with the freedom of human action, than the influence exerted by objects presented to the mind by the senses, or by the reasonings and persuasions of our fellow-men; and to him to whom nothing can be difficult, since the resources of his power and wisdom are infinite and inexhaustible, there can be no more difficulty in overruling the agency of devils, than in overruling the agency of wicked men, to the promotion of the great ends of his righteous and benignant government.

These remarks go no farther, and were intended to go no farther, than to show that the doctrine of the existence and agency of evil spirits is not, abstractly considered, an absurd tenet; that the attempt to put it down by ridicule, is altogether unworthy of men who lay claim to the honourable appellation of philosophers, lovers of wisdom; and that there is no necessity to have recourse to metaphor and allegory to explain away those passages of Scripture which, in their obvious and literal sense, explicitly teach this doctrine.

The evidence of the existence and agency of evil spirits is to be sought for in the Holy Scriptures. It is entirely a matter of supernatural revelation; and I have no hesitation in asserting, that such evidence is to be found there in such abundance and explicitness, that an unprejudiced reader, who believes the authenticity and inspiration of the sacred volume, and interprets its declarations on the principles which he applies to written language generally, will find it as difficult to doubt of the existence and doings of such a being as Satan or the devil, and his subordinate agents, as of the existence and doings of such men as Moses and Samuel, Peter or Paul.

The passage before us is one, out of a multitude, which clearly proves the existence and wide extent of malignant spiritual agency; and, in common with the most of such passages, shows that this doctrine is, like the doctrines of revelation generally, not a mere matter of curiosity or speculation, but calculated and intended to exert a powerful and a salutary influence, in forming the character and guiding the conduct of Christians during their present disciplinary and pre-paratory state. The fact is distinctly asserted, that the 'devil, their adversary, as a roaring lion, walketh about, seeking whom he may devour.' This asser-tion is made, that they may be induced to resist him; and, that in order to their successfully resisting him, they may be sober, and watchful, and steadfast in the faith; and they are encouraged, under the sufferings in which the attempts of their powerful, and crafty, and cruel, and active adversary may involve them, by the consideration, that such sufferings have been the common lot of the faithful in all ages, that they have been enabled to endure them, and in due season have been delivered from them, and by the promise of a divine support under, and a glorious triumph over, them. To these interesting topics, then, it is my intention to turn your minds, in the remaining part of the discourse. The Christian's adversary; the Christian's duty in reference to this adversary; and the Christian's encouragement while engaged in performing this duty.

PART I.

THE CHRISTIAN'S GREAT ENEMY

L et us first, then, consider the statement made respecting the Christian's adversary. 'Your adversary, the devil, as a roaring lion, walketh about, seeking whom he may devour.' There are two questions which here require attention. Who is this adversary? and what is here stated in reference to him?

1. Who is he? The devil.

To the first question, who is this adversary? the answer is, he is 'the devil.' The word translated 'devil,' properly signifies accuser, slanderer, calumniator, and is given to the chief of evil spirits as an appropriate designation. The same being is termed 'satan,' a word of similar meaning with devil, signifying enemy or accuser; 'the wicked one,' to mark his depravity generally, and especially his malignity; 'belial,' a term signifying low, abject, describing both his character and situation; 'the tempter;' 'the god and the prince of this world;' 'the chief of the demons;' 'beelzebub,' the lord of the flies; 'the prince of the power of the air;' 'apollyon,' the destroyer; 'he that hath the power of death;' 'the great dragon;' and 'the old serpent.'[1]

With regard to this very remarkable being, our information, all of course derived from revelation, though very limited, is abundantly distinct. He is a being of the angelic order, formed, as all intelligent beings were, and must have been, in a state of moral integrity, who, at a period anterior to the fall of man, in consequence of violating the Divine law, in a manner of which we are not informed, was, along with a large number of other spirits, who, it would appear, in consequence of being seduced by him, were partakers of his guilt, cast out of heaven, his 'original abode,' placed in a state of degradation and punishment, and reserved to deeper shame and fiercer pains 'at the day of the revelation of the righteous judgment of God.' Through his malignity and falsehood, man, who was innocent, became guilty; man, who was holy, became depraved; man, who was happy, became miserable; man, who was immortal, became liable to death.

Over the minds of the human race, while they continue irregenerate, he exercises a very powerful, though not physically irresistible influence, 'working in the children of disobedience, and leading them captive at his will;' and even over their bodies, he has

[1] *1 Chron.* 21:1, *Job* 1:6, *Eph.* 6:16, *2 Cor.* 6:15, *Matt* 4:5, *1 Thess.* 3:5, *2 Cor.* 4:4, *John* 12:31, *Matt.* 12:24, *Eph.* 2:2, *Rev.* 9:11, *Heb.* 2:14, *Rev.* 12:3, 9.

in many instances exercised a malignant power. He exerts himself, by his numerous agents, infernal and human, in counteracting the Divine benignant plan for the salvation of men. Error, sin, and misery, in all their forms, are, ultimately, his work; his animating principle is hatred of God, and his leading object the maintenance and extension of the power of evil.

During that period of holy light and happiness, the millennium, to which the church and the world have so long looked forward with eager desire, his power and opportunities to do evil will be greatly diminished, if not entirely taken away. In the period immediately preceding the general judgment, he will again manifest his unchanged hostility to the benignant designs of God respecting man; and when the mystery of God is finished, will, along with those angels and men who have chosen him for their leader in preference to God, be cut off forever from all intercourse with the unfallen and restored part of the intelligent creation, and 'punished with everlasting destruction from the presence of the Lord, and the glory of his power' (2 *Thess.* 1:9).

2. *What is he?*

(i.) He is an *adversary*—their adversary

Let us now inquire, in the second place, what is said of this extraordinary being in the passage before us. He is the Christian's adversary; 'your adversary the devil.' He is 'the adversary;' the friend of none, the enemy of all. Enmity, malignity, is the very element of his moral being. He hates God, and men, and holy angels; and the only tie apparently existing between him and his subordinate agents, is a common enmity against God, and all that is God's. He is the adversary of all men. He has deeply injured the race; and he does not pity, but hate, those whom he has injured. Murderer, manslayer, is his name from the beginning.[1]

But he is peculiarly the adversary of that portion of mankind, who have been led by the good Spirit to revolt from his usurped dominion, to place themselves under the guidance of the Captain of the Lord's host, and to become fellow-workers under him in the accomplishment of his great enterprise, which is 'to destroy the works of the devil.' Both as individuals and as a body, true Christians are the objects of the peculiar enmity of the evil one. This is the truth which is taught us in the Apocalypse, when we are told, that 'the dragon persecuted the woman who was clothed with the sun, and had the moon under her feet, and upon her head a crown of twelve stars; being wroth with her, and making war with the remnant of her seed, which keep the commandments of God, and have the testimony of Jesus Christ.' 'They were,' as Archbishop Leighton says, 'once under his power;

---

[1] *John* 8:44. ἀνθρωποκτόνος

and now, being escaped from him, he pursues them, as Pharaoh with all his forces, as a prey that was once in his den, and under his paw; and now that it is rescued, he rages and roars after it.' His object is the destruction of the Christian cause; the cause of truth and holiness, of God's glory and man's happiness; and therefore he cannot but be the adversary of those who seek to promote that cause. He exerts himself, by craft or violence, to induce them to abandon that cause, by doing which their sharing his destruction would be secured; or, if he cannot succeed in this object, he endeavours to make as miserable as he can in this world, those whom he knows he will have no opportunity of tormenting in the next.

Of the manner in which their adversary manifests his enmity to them, we have a very picturesque account in these words, 'As a roaring lion, he walketh about seeking whom he may devour.' Under the influence of inflamed malignity, which will not let him rest, compared to the lion's appetite for blood, sharpened by hunger, he, in the exercise of his power and craft, both of which are indicated by the figure, the lion being at once strong and wily, is constantly endeavouring to do them mischief. It is highly probable that the apostle had immediately in his eye the attempts which the wicked one was then making, by means of his agents, both infernal and human, to produce those fearful persecutions on the part of the Roman pagan empire, by which the faith and patience of the saints were so severely tried, by which multitudes were induced to make shipwreck of faith and a good conscience; turning back to perdition, becoming his prey, body and soul, forever. And multitudes more, who were faithful to the death, and obtained a crown of life, were, 'by the devil, cast into prison, and suffered tribulation:' 'they had trial of cruel mockings and scourgings: they were stoned, they were slain by the sword; they wandered about in sheep-skins and goat-skins; being destitute, afflicted, tormented; they wandered in deserts and in mountains, and in dens and in caves of the earth.' While I have little doubt that this is the immediate reference of the words, they bring before the mind certain general truths respecting our great spiritual enemy, of which it is of great importance that Christians, in all countries and ages, should be habitually mindful. They lead us to think of him as subtle, active, cruel, and powerful.

(ii.) He is a *subtle* adversary

This passage leads us to think of our great adversary as subtle. The lion, like all other beasts of prey, is endowed with a high degree of sagacity, to enable it to discover and surprise its prey. When David would convey to our minds an idea of the cunning of his enemies, he compares them to the lion. 'He sitteth in the lurking-places of the villages: in the secret places doth he murder the innocent: his eyes are privily set against the poor. He lieth in wait secretly as a lion in his den: he lieth in wait to catch the poor: he doth catch the poor, when he draweth him into his net. He croucheth, and humbleth himself, that the poor may fall by his strong ones.'[1] The figure naturally thus suggests the idea of subtlety. This is one of the leading thoughts, too, suggested, when the devil is represented as the old serpent: for 'the serpent was more subtle than any beast of the field which the Lord God had made.'

Subtlety is one of the most striking characters of our great spiritual enemy. He originally belonged to that order of beings whose wisdom is proverbial—'wise as an angel of God;' and, when he lost his moral purity, we have no reason to think he lost his intellectual energy. It took a new direction, but with unabated force. From the change of its object, it ceased indeed to deserve the name of wisdom. The appropriate appellation henceforward was craft or subtlety. We have a melancholy proof of his cunning, in the method he followed in his successful attempt to deceive the mother of mankind. With what consummate address does he whet her curiosity, quiet her fears, and flatter her vanity, till he has accomplished his great purpose, the ruin of our race! Ever since he obtained that victory over our first parents, he has been engaged in tempting their children; and the experience of nearly six thousand years, added to

---

[1] *Psa.* 10:8-10.

his natural cunning, must have rendered him expert indeed in the art of deceiving, that he may destroy. Accordingly, we find the apostle terming those suggestions, by which he endeavours to lead men astray from God, 'the wiles, the devices of the devil.'[1]

He has no power indeed of obtaining directly a knowledge of the human heart. That is the peculiar prerogative of him who made it. 'I the Lord search the heart, I try the reins.'[2] But he carefully observes our conduct, and shrewdly draws conclusions respecting our prevailing dispositions. His temptations are regulated by the information he thus obtains. He suits the snare to the habits of the bird he means to entrap. He draws the voluptuary[3] into the way of iniquity by the lure of pleasure, the avaricious by the promise of gain, the ambitious by the prospect of glory. He goes round about his victims, that he may espy where is the quarter in which they are weakest, or least afraid of attack, that he may assault them there. He takes advantage of everything in their temper, age, and condition, to give effect to his suggestions.

He keeps himself as much as possible out of view, and manages his approaches so as, that when danger is at length apprehended, there is scarce a possibility of escape. He even occasionally transforms

---

[1] *Eph.* 6:11.

[2] *Jer.* 17:10.

[3] A person whose life is devoted to the pursuit and enjoyment of luxury and sensual pleasure.

himself into an angel of light, and employs as his instruments, often while they themselves are unaware of it, the very persons from whom we would have been the last to suspect any hazard.

Sometimes he gets possession of the citadel of the heart as it were by storm, without allowing opportunity or time for repelling the assault. At other times he proceeds by sap[1] and mine; and, without alarm to the conscience, effects his nefarious purpose. But it were endless to enumerate all the subtle devices by which Satan endeavours to disturb the peace and retard the progress of the saint; to prevent the repentance, and to secure the destruction of the sinner. Enough has been said to show, that the figure chosen by the sacred writer is in this respect a significant one; and that the lion, in his arts for securing his prey, is a truly, but an imperfectly, descriptive emblem of 'him who beguileth Eve through his subtlety,' and has deluded, and is deluding, so many millions of her sons into those ways of error and sin which lead down to the chambers of eternal death.

(iii.) He is an *active* adversary

But our great spiritual enemy is not only subtle, he is also active. The lion ranges far and near in quest of his prey. The lion of hell is here represented as walking about, seeking whom he may devour. 'Whence comest thou?' said Jehovah to Satan, when he, as

---

[1] A concealed trench.

the accuser of the brethren, appeared in the midst of the sons of God. 'Whence comest thou?' The answer was, 'From going to and fro through the earth, and from walking up and down in it.'[1] The malignant exertions of the wicked one seem to be unintermitted. Langour and fatigue appear to be feelings to which he is a stranger. In the book of Revelation, he is represented as 'accusing the brethren before God, day and night.'[2] He is probably the more assiduous in his labours of malignity, as he knows that the period for his active exertions is limited. We cannot doubt that he is aware of the doom that awaits him; that, after a fixed term of ages, he is to be cast into the lake of fire, in the abyss of woe, and kept there under chains, which no created power can, which the uncreated power will not, unloose for ever. He has nothing approaching to satisfaction but in propagating sin and misery; and he knows that this is to come to a close. 'The devil is come down among men, having great wrath, knowing that his time is short,' or limited.[3]

In realising to our minds the activity of our great spiritual foe, we are not to think of him merely as an individual. No doubt he is a very active being; but this is not all. He is the chief and prince of unnumbered depraved spirits, who own his authority, prosecute his designs, and obey his commands. Their

[1] *Job* 1:7.
[2] *Rev.* 12:10.
[3] *Rev.* 12:12.

name is legion; for there are many of them. This gives him a species of ubiquity, and enables him to do what no individual created power and activity could accomplish.

His operations are often really continued when they seem to be intermitted. The mode of conducting them is changed, but the work is not abandoned; and, if he does suspend them for a season, it is but that he may recommence them with a greater probability of success. This remark holds both with respect to those who are yet his willing slaves, and to those who have escaped from under his thrall. 'When the unclean spirit goeth out of a man, he walketh through dry places, seeking rest, but finding none. Then he saith, I will return again to my house from whence I came out; and when he is come, he finds this empty, swept, and garnished. Then goeth he, and taketh with him seven other spirits more wicked than himself, and they enter in and dwell there: and the last state of that man is worse than the first.'[1] We have an instance of his returning to renew his attack with redoubled violence on those over whom he has no power, in the case of our Lord. We read, after the temptation of forty days in the wilderness, that 'the devil departed from him;' but it was only in that form, and but 'for a season.'[2] He was still going about him, seeking an occasion to make attack on

[1] *Matt.* 12:43-45.
[2] *Luke* 4:13.

him; and we find him in the hour of exhaustion and sorrow springing on his victim, and by his infernal assault drawing forth from the lips of him who was embodied patience and fortitude, those awful words, as if all he had experienced of diabolical attacks hitherto were unworthy of notice, 'Now is the hour and power of darkness.'

(iv.) He is a *cruel* adversary

Cruelty is another feature in the character of our great spiritual enemy, which the statement in the text brings before the mind. The lion is a stranger to pity. Like most ravenous beasts, he seems to have satisfaction in inflicting pain. The bleating of the lamb whom he is about to devour awakens in him no relentings, and he regards not the agonies he occasions to the bleeding, mangled sufferer. Equally ruthless is the great murderer from the beginning, the great destroyer of human souls. He appears to have a savage satisfaction in producing misery. The lion, when he tears to pieces the quivering limbs of the slaughtered kid, has an enjoyment altogether separate from the gratification of the desire to destroy. He satisfies the painful cravings of hunger, and obtains nourishment for his body. But the destroyer of human innocence and peace, the devourer of souls, derives no advantage, can derive no advantage, knows that he can derive no advantage, from the miseries which he inflicts, the ruin which he occasions. On the contrary, every malignant act deepens his guilt, and will aggravate his future condemnation; and he cannot but be aware of this. Yet so deeply is the desire of diffusing misery rooted in his nature, that though conscious that in yielding to it, he is but rendering his miserable condition more miserable, 'treasuring up to himself wrath against the day of wrath and revelation of the righteous judgment of God,'[1] he still, day and night, restlessly seeks for opportunities of making the good bad, and the bad worse, the happy miserable, and the miserable more miserable.

(v.) He is a *powerful* adversary

The only other idea suggested by the figurative description of our great spiritual enemy is, that he is a being of formidable power. Solomon informs us that the 'lion is the strongest among beasts,'[2] and, I believe modern naturalists hold that there is no animal of the same size which possesses so much muscular power. The devil belongs to an order, the angelic, which excels in strength; and though we know his powers are restrained by the Divine providence, we have no reason to think that his moral depravation produced any diminution of his physical energy. The tempest which overwhelmed the family of Job in the ruins of the house of their elder brother, and the fearful effects produced both on the bodies and the minds of

[1] *Rom.* 2:5.
[2] *Prov.* 30:30.

those individuals who were the subjects of demoniac possession, prove both what he can do, and would do, if not restrained by a superior power. To what extent he can and does employ physical agents, what are commonly termed the powers of nature, in executing his malignant designs, we cannot tell. This we know, that the Scripture representations naturally lead us to think of Satan as not weak, but powerful. He is emblematized in the parable by 'the strong man;' and the apostle obviously estimates those unseen opponents, of whom the devil is the leader, as far more formidable foes than the most powerful human enemies.

We need, according to him, divine strength and heavenly armour to resist such enemies. 'Be strong,' says he, 'in the Lord and in the power of his might. Put on the whole armour of God, that ye may be able to stand against the wiles of the devil: for we wrestle not against flesh and blood, but against principalities and powers, against the rulers of the darkness of this world, against spiritual wickedness in high places.'[1] So much for illustration of the apostle's statement respecting the Christian's great spiritual enemy, so subtle, so active, so cruel, so powerful.

That part of our subject which we have attempted to illustrate, is replete with important practical instruction.

[1] *Matt.* 12:29, *Eph.* 6:10-12.

What a striking view does the contrast of the original and the present character and employment of the devil, give us of the malignant nature and tremendous power of moral evil! He who is now the worst and the most miserable of created beings, was once one of the best and the happiest. He who now prowls about the universe, 'a fugitive and a vagabond,' restless and miserable everywhere, had his first abode in the region of perfect purity, near to the throne of the Eternal; and, instead of as now going about seeking how he can waste and destroy the best part of God's works, his constant employment and delight was to celebrate the praises and do the commandments of Jehovah, hearkening to the voice of his word. And what has effected the fearful change? What has converted the angel into the devil? It was sin; that only evil in God's universe in which there is no good; that evil, the depths of whose malignity no created mind can sound. Man in his fallen state compared with man in his primeval state, earth in its present state compared with paradise, strikingly show that it is an evil and a bitter thing to depart from God; but still more striking is the illustration we have of this most important truth, when we contrast the accursed fiend with the holy angel, and the bottomless pit and the fiery lake with the palace of the great king, the Lord of Hosts, and the rivers of pleasure that are at his right hand for evermore.

How disgraceful and miserable must be the condition of those who are the slaves of this subtle, active, cruel, powerful, depraved intelligence, in turns the instruments of his detestable designs and the victims of his insatiable cruelty! And this is the situation of all unconverted men, whether they are aware of it or not. They are of their father the devil; and his lusts—the things he desires and delights in—they willingly abuse their powers and degrade their nature in doing. They are 'taken captive by him at his will.'[1] He is their successful tempter now. He will be, if mercy prevent not, their unrelenting tormentor forever. Oh, that they were aware of the horrors of their situation, that they saw its debasement, that they felt its wretchedness, that they realised its dangers!

How grateful should we be to him who came to destroy the works of the wicked one, and to deliver men from his usurped dominion and baleful power! The house of the strong man has been entered by one stronger than he. The prey has been taken from the mighty, and the captive of the terrible one delivered. The greatness of the blessing, apart from the manner in which it was procured, calls for lively gratitude; but the claims of our deliverer are felt to be tenfold strong, when we recollect that he, the only begotten, the Holy One, of God, submitted to be tempted of the devil, to have the moral sensibilities of his holy

[1] *2 Tim.* 2:26.

22

nature shocked and tortured by his loathsome suggestions, that we might be delivered from his power, and be taught, by the example of 'the Captain of our salvation,' how to conduct the conflict with the enemy, so as to become more than conquerors through him who loved us. Blessed, ever blessed, be he who came in the name of the Lord to bruise the head of the old serpent; and who, through the merit of his atonement and the power of his Spirit, enables the most feeble and timid of his people to 'tread on the lion and the adder,' and to 'trample the young lion and the dragon under foot.'

Let Christians rejoice that, if a subtle, cruel, active, and powerful enemy is continually prowling about, the eye of infinite wisdom and love rests ever on them, the arm of never-tiring omnipotence is ever around them to protect and defend them. The lion of hell is a chained lion, a muzzled lion, to Christians. He may alarm, but he shall never devour them. His chain is in the hand of his conqueror and their Lord. It was very natural for Peter to put his brethren in mind of their great enemy. He must have often thought of the words of our Lord Jesus, 'Simon, Simon, Satan hath desired to have you, that he may sift you as wheat; but I have prayed for thee, that thy faith fail not.'[1] His experience is full of warning and encouragement. It proves that if Christians

---

[1] *Luke* 22:31, 32.

are not cautious, though the lion of hell shall not be permitted to devour them, he may inflict wounds of which they will bear the marks till the close of life; and it finely illustrates our Lord's declaration,— 'I give unto my sheep eternal life, and they shall never perish; neither shall any pluck them out of my hand.' Neither their own heedlessness, nor the malignity of their infernal foe, shall be able to accomplish their destruction. Let him, then, that is born of God, 'keep himself, that the wicked one touch him not;'[1] and let his joy, that he has a better keeper than himself, even the keeper of Israel, who never slumbers nor sleeps, not produce security, but encourage vigilance. God keeps his people, not without but through their own watchfulness.

Finally, let all of us who have reason to hope that we have been emancipated from the powers of the wicked one, in our humble station co-operate with our great Deliverer in rescuing our fellow-men from the degrading bondage, from the destroying power, of his and our great enemy; and while the children of the devil are so clearly proving themselves to be so, by imitating him in going about seeking whom they may destroy, let us prove our connection with him whom we claim as our Lord and Master, by going about doing good, endeavouring to pluck the brand from the burning, to pull the prey of the lion of hell

[1] *John* 10:28, *1 John* 5:18.

from his devouring jaws, to seek and to save what is in extreme hazard, through the craft and activity, the power and cruelty, of the wicked one, of being lost, lost forever.

PART II.

THE CHRISTIAN'S DUTY
IN REFERENCE TO HIS GREAT ENEMY

L et us now consider the apostle's account of the Christian's duty in reference to his great spiritual adversary. His duty is to resist him; and, in order effectually to resist him, to be sober, to be watchful, to be steadfast in the faith.

1. What he must do to his great enemy—resist him

The attacks of our great spiritual enemy naturally divide themselves into two classes; those which are made on the Christian as an individual, and those which are made on the christian cause. It is the duty of the Christian to resist both.

(i.) He must resist his attacks *on himself*

Temptation to sin is the manner in which the evil one attacks the individual Christian. Sometimes these temptations are direct; oftener they are indirect; but all temptation to sin, like all sin itself, may be considered as directly or indirectly the work of the devil.

It is much more a matter of curiosity than of use, to seek to distinguish accurately the temptations which come immediately from the wicked one, from those in presenting which to the mind he employs intermediate agencies. But it is of great importance to remember, that all solicitations to sin, from whatever quarter they come, are in accordance with his will, and, if not resisted, will contribute to the gaining of his object in warring against the soul. Of all suggestions of this kind, we may say both that they come not, they cannot come, from above; they do, they must, come from beneath. Of some of them we may say they are 'earthly,' of others they are 'sensual,' of all they are 'devilish.'

Generally speaking, it is the duty of the Christian carefully to keep out of the way of temptation, to avoid everything, which can be avoided in consistency with duty, which may afford an opportunity to the great enemy or his agents to assail him with solicitations to sin. It is madness to hold parley with him, or uncalled on to provoke him to combat. Such unnecessary tamperings, such self-confident conflicts, generally end in sin and shame.

But the adversary will not let the Christian alone, and the path of duty is a path that sometimes, indeed ofttimes, leads into temptation. When the Christian is attacked, he must not flee, he must not yield himself up into the hands of his enemy; he must resist, he must oppose him. He must not comply with his solicitations. Like that good spiritual soldier of ancient times he must say, 'How can I do this great wickedness and sin against God?' or, like the Captain of salvation, he must, with the shield of faith, quench all the fiery darts of the wicked, repelling his reiterated suggestions by 'It is written, it is written,' and in holy indignation bidding him 'get behind him.'[1] He must not allow himself to deliberate on a proposal which involves in it the denial of truth, the neglect of duty, or the commission of sin, by whatever plausibilities and apparent advantages it may be recommended, but immediately, and with abhorrence, reject it.

Non-compliance with the suggestions of the wicked one, is, however, but a part of the Christian duty of resistance. The Christian must oppose the wicked one. He must not merely stand on the defensive; he must attack the enemy, he must quit himself like a man, and so fight as to turn to flight the alien and his armies. He must so resist the devil as that he shall flee from him. In plain words, he must make solicitations to sin occasions and means of progress in holiness. For example, when tempted to fretfulness under affliction, instead of yielding to the temptation, he must 'glorify God in the fires,' by more than ever possessing his soul in patience, and counting it all joy to be brought into manifold tribulation. When tempted to

[1] *Matt.* 4:4, 7, 10.

be ashamed of Christ or his cause, he must seize that opportunity of making his conduct proclaim more loudly than ever, 'God forbid that I should glory, save in the cross of our Lord Jesus Christ.' When tempted to penuriousness in supporting the cause of Christ, he must give more cheerfully, and, if possible, more plenteously, than ever. When tempted to be weary in well-doing, he must feel this as a powerful reason why he should be 'steadfast and immovable, always abounding in the work of the Lord.' When tempted to associate with the worldly and ungodly, he should take an opportunity of showing that in the saints on the earth, the excellent ones, is all his delight. When tempted to draw very near the borders of criminal indulgence, let him not even stand still where he is, but retire still farther from the appearance of evil, and carefully keep off 'the debatable land.' When the evil one tempts to unfrequency or carelessness in sacred prayer, let it be felt as a reason why he should seek to realise more and more in his own experience, what it is to 'pray in the spirit, to pray always, with all prayer and supplication, and to watch thereunto with all perseverance.' Let temptations to carelessness produce increased vigilance, and to indolence increased diligence. Let attempts to make us neglect the assembling of ourselves together, lead to more conscientious attendance on public religious services, and more undivided attention in them. In one word, let all his endeavours to lead us in the way of sin, end in our farther advancement in the opposite way of holiness. This is the way to turn the artillery of the wicked one against himself. Nothing is so well fitted to mortify that old adversary, as to find that the very means he employs to produce our apostasy and ruin are converted into the occasion of our establishment in the faith, our advancement in holiness, and our fitness for heaven. So much for the resistance which the Christian is to make to the attacks of his great spiritual enemy, directed immediately against himself as an individual.

(ii.) He must resist his attacks on the *Christian cause*

But the Christian is to resist not only these attacks, he is to resist also the attacks which his adversary the devil is constantly making on the cause of Christ. He is constantly engaged in endeavouring to corrupt the truth as it is in Jesus; to introduce, and maintain, and extend error, and superstition, and fanaticism, and schism, and bigotry, and disorder, and impurity, in the churches of Christ, and to oppose the exertions which are making to diffuse the knowledge and the influence of 'the truth and grace, which came by Jesus Christ.' The Christian is to fight against Satan, not only in his own heart, but in the church and the world. There is a battle-field without as well as within. He is carefully to avoid everything which may in any way prove, however unintentionally, co-operation with the lawless one in his nefarious designs; and by

THE CHRISTIAN'S GREAT ENEMY

all proper methods he must endeavour to counteract him.

He must, however, take care not to attempt what has been too frequently attempted, to vanquish the wicked one by weapons borrowed from his own armoury, he must not repel force by force, false argument by false argument, railing by railing. In such conflict the devil is sure to overcome; indeed, the very employment of these weapons is a proof that he has already, to a certain degree, overcome. In this warfare, Christians must remember that 'the weapons of their warfare are not carnal, but mighty through God to the pulling down strongholds, and bringing into captivity every high thought that exalteth itself against the knowledge of God.' Their motto must be, 'Not by might and power, but by God's Spirit.' 'By pureness, by knowledge, by long-suffering, by kindness, by the Holy Ghost, by love unfeigned, by the word of truth, by the power of God, by the armour of righteousness on the right hand and the left.' This is the manner in which the apostle teaches us to carry on our warfare for the cause of Christ against the cause of the devil. 'The servant of God must not strive, but be gentle to all men, apt to teach, patient, in meekness instructing those who oppose themselves, if God, peradventure, will give them repentance to the acknowledging of the truth, and that they may deliver themselves out of the snare of the devil, who are taken captive of him at his will.'[1]

Christians are not to stand looking idly on when the wicked one, by ignorance and error, and superstition and profligacy, is consummating the eternal perdition of men by millions. No, they are to 'rise up for God against the evil-doer, they are to stand up for Him against' his armies, 'the workers of iniquity.' As 'the armies of heaven, clothed in fine linen, white and clean,'[2] they are to follow on their white horses him whose name is the Word of God, faithful and true, who, clothed in a vesture dipt in blood, rides forth prosperously on his white horse, 'in righteousness, judging and making war, conquering and to conquer.' Like him, wherever they are, according to the facilities afforded by their circumstances, they are to be constantly engaged in destroying the works of the devil. Thus, then, are Christians to resist their adversary the devil.[3]

---

[1] 2 *Cor.* 10:4, *Zech.* 4:6, 2 *Cor.* 6:6-8, 2 *Tim* 2:24-26.

[2] *Rev.* 19:11-14.

[3] The motives to resistance are strongly put by Tertullian: '*Stat conflictus conspector, et victoriae Agonothetes, Deus vivus: Xystarches, Spiritus Sanctus: Epistates, Christus Jesus; Corona, aeternitatis brabium, angelicae in coelis substantiae politia, gloria in secula seculorum.*'—*Lib. ad martyr*, iii. [Translation: 'There is established as watcher over the conflict and judge of victory the living God; as manager the Holy Spirit; as superintendent Jesus Christ; and for the crown there is the prize of eternity, citizenship of angelic substance in the heavens and glory for eternity.']

2. What the Christian is to do, that he may resist his great enemy

The apostle not only enjoins this duty of resistance, he also instructs Christians how they are to be enabled to perform it. If they would successfully resist the devil, either in their own hearts, or in the church and the world, they must 'be sober, vigilant, and steadfast in the faith.' Let us shortly explain these exercises, and show how necessary they are, and how well fitted they are, to enable the Christian to resist his adversary the devil.

When we read these words, we feel that the injunctions contained in them have already been given; the first of them more than once. The reiteration of such precepts in so short an epistle, teaches a lesson both to ministers and people, both to the teachers and the taught. It says to the first, 'for you to say the same things should not be grievous,' for the second, 'it is safe;' ay, it is necessary 'Precept must be on precept, line upon line; here a little, and there a little.' 'It were easy,' says Archbishop Leighton, 'to entertain men's mind with new discourse, if our task were rather to please than to profit; for there be many things which, with little labour, might be brought forth as new and strange to ordinary hearers. But there be a few things which it chiefly concerns us to know and practise, and these are to be more frequently represented and pressed. This apostle, and other divine writers, drew from too full a spring to be ebb of matter; but they rather choose profitable iterations[1] than unprofitable variety, and so should we.' Yet we shall find that, though substantially the same exhortations are repeated, it is always with a peculiar adaptation to the connection in which they occur. They are not mere repetitions; they are examples of the applications of general principles, or precepts, to particular cases. It is obviously so in the instance before us.

(i.) He must be *sober*

The word here translated 'be sober,' is the same which, in the seventh verse of the preceding chapter, is rendered be vigilant. Its proper signification is to be abstinent from, or temperate in the use of, wine or other intoxicating drinks. It designates a state directly the reverse of a state of intoxication. The word may be understood either literally or figuratively. If understood literally, we are here taught that temperance, in reference to intoxicating drinks, is necessary in order to our resisting the devil. And, certainly, nothing can be more obviously true than this. The natural tendency of intoxicating drinks is to diminish the power of conscience and reason, and to increase the power of the lower principles of our nature, animal appetite and irascible feeling. It increases the strength of what needs to be restrained, and weakens the strength of what is fitted and intended to restrain.

[1] Directions.

It delivers the man, in one point of view, bound hand and foot, so far as resistance is concerned, into the devil's hands; and, in another, presents him a willing soldier, appropriately armed for his service. An intoxicated man would be ill-fitted to take care of himself, if exposed to the attacks of subtle, powerful beasts of prey; and he is certainly not better fitted to guard himself against that crafty and active, strong and cruel spiritual enemy, who is here represented as prowling about like a roaring lion. While this is undoubtedly true, and, highly important, as the corresponding term 'be vigilant,' that is, wakeful, is plainly to be understood in a figurative sense, we apprehend the expression before us, must also be interpreted figuratively; an interpretation which substantially includes the literal meaning, while it includes much more.

'Things seen and temporal,' the pleasures, the riches, the honours of this world, are apt to intoxicate the mind. Men under their supreme influence are regulated more by imagination and appetite than by conscience and reason. What is present and sensible, occupies the whole mind. What is unseen and future, is overlooked and forgotten, and treated as if it had no existence. Time is everything, eternity is nothing. This is mental intoxication; and sobriety, in opposition to this, is just the sound estimate which enlightened conscience and reason form of the comparative value of things seen and unseen, things temporal and eternal, with a habitual state of feeling and action corresponding to this estimate.

He is sober who reckons that the ever-enduring holy happiness which can be found only in possessing the favour, and being conformed to the image of God, is of more true value to man than all else which the created universe contains; that the certainty of attaining the greatest earthly good is too dearly purchased by the slightest hazard of losing this happiness; that no sacrifice, no suffering, is to be much counted on if necessary in order to its attainment; and that what has no tendency to secure this, cannot be a matter of very much importance to a being like man. Such a man shows a mind free from intoxication. He judges of things as they really are. His maxims are obviously the words of truth and soberness. God is more excellent than the creature. The soul is more valuable than the body. Heaven is better than earth, far better than hell. Time is shorter than eternity.

The man who is thus sober is prepared for resisting the devil, in both the ways illustrated above. The devil is the god of this world, and all his power is derived from it. The sum of what he has to say in the way of temptation is, 'All earthly good is delivered to me, and to whomsoever I will I give it. All earthly evil is in my power, and on whomsoever I will I inflict it.' It is by the hope of worldly good, or the fear of worldly evil, that he prevails on men to neglect duty, and to commit sin. But the truly sober man has his spiritual senses too well exercised to believe either the implied or the express falsehood. He knows that God has not relinquished the government of the world, or so committed it into the hands of his great enemy, as that he has the disposal either of the good or the evil of life; and though it were otherwise, he knows that there is a more valuable good which compliance with his suggestions would forfeit; a more dreadful evil to which compliance with his suggestions would expose him. So far as he is influenced by this sober judgment, he 'keeps himself, and the wicked one toucheth him not.' And the same sober judgments of the value of the soul, and of the importance of eternity, naturally lead to strenuous, persevering exertions to resist the devil, in his attempts to introduce error and superstition into the church, and to perpetuate ignorance, idolatry, and wickedness in the world.

(ii.) He must be *vigilant*

But that Christians may effectually resist their adversary the devil, the apostle calls on them to be not only sober, but 'vigilant.' The literal meaning of the word is in opposition to falling asleep, to keep awake as shepherds do when watching their sheep by night, or sentinels when keeping watch on the walls of a city; it indicates a state of watchfulness, in opposition to a state of sleep or drowsiness. Some would interpret the words literally; and it is on this ground, among others, that Roman Catholics prescribe watching as well as fasting as a means of spiritual advantage, and of successfully resisting our ghostly adversaries.

There can be no reasonable doubt, however, that here, and wherever else in the New Testament, watching is prescribed as a general christian duty, the word is used figuratively. A state of security, inattention, and inactivity, is naturally emblematized by a state of sleep; and a state of consciousness of existing hazards, attention to them, and active employment of the means to escape them, by a state of watching or wakefulness.

To be watchful, with a reference to the resistance of the evil one, implies that the individual is aware of the existence and reality of the hazards to which, from malignant spiritual influence, his highest interests are exposed; that he is on the alert to notice all the movements of the subtle, active, cruel, and powerful foe; and that not ignorant of, or inattentive to, his devices, he looks around him, walks circumspectly, aware that in any quarter the enemy may make his appearance; and that he so disguises himself, and varies his form, that it requires spiritual sagacity,[1] in its most awakened state, to detect him; and, finally, that when he does discover him ready to deceive or to devour, to delude or destroy, he is ready, broad awake, in full possession of his spiritual faculties, prepared to employ the proper means for counter-working him, and disappointing his nefarious purposes.

[1] Acuteness of mental discernment and soundness of judgment.

It is not enough that a man be sober, that is, not intoxicated, round whom a powerful crafty beast of prey is prowling. He must be wakeful. However sober, if he fall asleep, he is in imminent hazard of being dangerously wounded, if not devoured. Indeed, he is not acting like a sober man, if in these circumstances, he allows himself to fall asleep. In like manner, the Christian must not only have a just estimate of the transcendent importance of things unseen and eternal, but his spiritual senses must be habitually exercised; the eyes of his mind 'must look right on, and his eyelids look straight before him.' He must 'ponder the path of his feet,' and especially 'keep his heart with all diligence; for out of it are the issues of life.'[1] He must, like a watchful sentinel, take good heed, that through none of the external senses, the gates, as Bunyan represents them, of the good town Mansoul, the great adversary, under any disguise, find his way to the citadel of the heart. He must be watchful, for his enemy is so.

The influence which this vigilance is calculated to exert on the resistance of the wicked one in his attack both on us as individuals, and on the cause of Christ, is so obvious, that I may safely leave you to follow out this train of thought in your private meditations.

[1] *Prov.* 4:23, 25, 26.

(iii.) He must be *steadfast in the faith*

The third and principal means by which Christians are to be enabled to resist the great adversary, is the being 'steadfast in the faith.' We call that the principal means; for it is as necessary to the right use of the other means as to the gaining of the common end: as necessary to the being 'sober and vigilant' as to 'the resisting of the devil.'

The apostle takes for granted that the persons whom he addressed were 'believers.' They were 'in the faith;' and he calls on them to be 'steadfast in the faith.' Had he been speaking to unconverted men, the first thing he would have called on them to do, would have been to believe; for, till they believed, they could neither see their danger, nor use the means which were necessary for their safety. They to whom he writes had believed the truth respecting their natural condition as the willing, helpless slaves of the wicked one, bound in the fetters of guilt and the cords of depravity. They had believed the truth respecting Jesus the great deliverer, who, by the blood of his covenant, had made provision for the deliverance of the prisoners out of the pit in which there was no water; who proclaims liberty to the captive, and the opening of the prison doors to them who are bound; who takes the prey from the mighty, and delivers the captive of the terrible one. They had believed that those who refuse to be released by him, must, along with their enslaver, be shut up under everlasting chains in the prison of hell, and that they who accept of the freely offered deliverance shall, under the protection and guidance of their redeeming Lord, be preserved, amid all the attempts of their former oppressors to bring them again into slavery, and ultimately be placed by him in circumstances of perfect, holy happiness, while Satan shall be forever bruised under their feet.

It is the belief of these things that has sobered their minds, and roused them to spiritual vigilance. This has wakened them, and it is this only that can keep them awake; and for this purpose they must be 'steadfast in the faith.' They must hold fast the truth as it is in Jesus.

It is not enough that they have believed; they must continue believing. The truth and its evidence must be habitually before their minds. Everything depends on that. They are safe 'if they keep in memory what has been preached to them;' not otherwise. The truth works effectually towards the resistance of the wicked one, but only in him who believes it, and only in the degree in which he believes it. It is faith that makes the Christian strong for combat. Let him lose sight of the truth and its evidence, and, like Samson shorn of his locks, he is weak as another man. Whenever he staggers through unbelief, he becomes powerless in resisting the great adversary. It is he only who puts on the whole armour of God that can stand in the evil day; but it is the believer alone who can put on and wear and wield that armour. It is the girdle of truth believed that can alone gird up the loins of the mind. The breastplate is the righteousness which is of God by faith. The well-roughed shoes, of the preparation of the gospel of peace, which are necessary to enable the spiritual soldier to stand firm in the slippery field of temptation, can be worn only by them who believe that gospel. The shield, which enables him to quench all the fiery darts of the wicked one, is the shield of faith. The hope, which is the helmet of salvation, can grace no brow but the brow of the believer, for hope rests on faith; the sword of the Spirit, which is the word of God, can be wielded only by the arm of the believer; and the prayer which is necessary to secure the right and the effectual use of all those pieces of spiritual armour, is the prayer of faith.

Had our first parents been steadfast in faith, they had never fallen. They became the prey of unbelief in the shape of doubt, before they became the victims of the devil. God said, 'Ye shall surely die;' they doubted him. The devil said, 'Ye shall not surely die;' they believed him: and then were befooled and enslaved by him. It was by being steadfast in faith that the great Captain of our salvation successfully resisted the wicked one, and blunted all his fiery darts. To them all he presented the shield of faith in a specific Divine declaration, and the most envenomed of them fell harmless at his feet. By faith all the elders who have received a good report turned to flight the alien armies of their infernal as well as mortal enemies;

THE CHRISTIAN'S GREAT ENEMY

and still is it true, and it will continue true till the last spiritual conflict has taken place on earth, 'This is the victory that overcometh the world,' and the god of the world, 'even our faith.'[1] Here, as in the former case, I leave it to yourselves to follow out more fully the manner in which steadfast faith operates in enabling Christians to resist the adversary in his attacks on themselves individually, and on the great cause of their Lord and King.

[1] *1 John* 5:4.

PART III.

THE CHRISTIAN'S ENCOURAGEMENT TO PERFORM HIS DUTY IN REFERENCE TO HIS GREAT ENEMY

It only remains that we briefly attend to the encouragement which the Christian has amid the sufferings in which his struggles with his spiritual enemies may involve him. That encouragement is derived from two sources—an undoubted fact and a faithful promise; an undoubted fact—the same struggle has been sustained and surmounted by all the brotherhood: and a faithful promise—'the God of all grace, who hath called them unto his eternal glory by Christ Jesus, after they have suffered a while, will make them perfect, stablish, strengthen, settle them.' Let us attend to these encouragements in their order.

1. The encouraging fact—all the brotherhood have sustained and surmounted this struggle

And first, let us consider the encouraging fact. 'Knowing this,' says the apostle, 'that the same afflictions are accomplished in your brethren who are in the world.' It has been questioned whether the sufferings here spoken of refer to the inward sufferings occasioned by the temptations of the wicked one, or to the outward sufferings, the persecutions which spring out of the influence of the wicked one on the minds of his slaves and their enemies. I do not think that it is necessary, or even proper, to confine it to either. It refers to sufferings growing out of the machinations and agency of their great spiritual adversary of whatever kind. The apostle states that 'the same afflictions'—afflictions of the same kind arising from the same cause—'were accomplished in their brethren,' literally, 'in their brotherhood,' 'in the world.'

Some have thought that these words contain in them but little to support under suffering, and have applied the words of a heathen moralist: 'It is but poor consolation that I am one of many sufferers.' But if we look at the words carefully, we shall find that they are replete with encouragement.

Sufferers are apt to think their case quite singular; others have been tried, but none tried as they are; and the Apostle Paul shows his knowledge of human nature when he says to the Corinthians, 'There hath no temptation taken you but such as is common to man.'[1] Your sufferings are not peculiar. It is unreasonable to complain of what is so common a lot. It were pusillanimous[2] to sink under what so many are suffering and have sustained.

---

[1] 1 *Cor.* 10:13.
[2] Lacking courage or resolution; cowardly; faint-hearted; timid.

But the consolation here given is of a higher kind than this. These sufferings are characteristic of the brotherhood to which you belong. Every member of that brotherhood is a partaker of them. He who is the first-born of the many brethren experienced the temptations of the devil and the persecutions of wicked men; and in their sufferings all the younger branches of the holy family have fellowship with him. You could not belong to that brotherhood if you were entire strangers to their afflictions.[1] 'If ye were of the world the world would love its own,' and the god of this world would not so attack you; 'but because ye are not of the world, but chosen out of the world,' therefore the world and its prince harass and abuse you. It is one of the family badges; 'if ye were without such chastisements,' of which all the children, all the brotherhood, are partakers, 'then were ye bastards, and not sons.'[2] Would you willingly part with the characteristic privileges of the brotherhood, in order to obtain exemption from their characteristic sufferings? Besides, as these sufferings are common to the brotherhood, you may be assured of that cordial sympathy which lightens suffering, and that 'fervent prayer which avails much.'

Then there is some peculiarity in the phrase 'are accomplished,' are fulfilled. It is not said they are

[1] '*Erras si putas, unquam Christianum persecutionem non pati.*'—*Hieronymus*. [Translation: You are wrong if you think there is ever a time when a Christian does not suffer persecution. (Jerome)]

[2] *John* 15:19, *Heb.* 12:8.

47

THE CHRISTIAN'S GREAT ENEMY

endured by, but they are accomplished or fulfilled in.
This peculiar mode of expression leads us to think
of these sufferings as appointments which must be
fulfilled. No chance has happened to you. 'This hath
come forth from him who is wonderful in counsel
and excellent in working.' Satan and his agents are
but doing to you, as they did to your Lord, 'what
God's hand and counsel before time determined to
be done.' These temptations and persecutions are a
part of the manifold trials to which, for a season, it
is needful that you be subject; for 'they who would
live godly in this world must suffer persecution.'
Your Lord has assured you, that 'in the world ye
shall have tribulation;' and his apostle, that 'through
much tribulation ye must enter the kingdom.' These
are sufferings to which ye are appointed and called.
These are sufferings appointed to every Christian as
a member of the body of Christ, and they must be
accomplished. They are a part of the discipline by
which the brotherhood on earth are to be made fit
for joining the brotherhood in heaven.

And, then, what encouragement and consolation
is there in the thought, that these afflictions, as they
must for wise and benignant reasons be endured by
the whole brotherhood while they are in the world,
are to be accomplished here? The brotherhood, who
are with their Father and their elder Brother in heav-
en, are completely beyond the reach of temptation
and persecution. Satan is bruised under their feet.

They are made more than conquerors. The helmet has been exchanged for the crown that fadeth not away; the sword of conflict for the palm of victory; and the cry, 'I am oppressed, undertake for me,' for the shout, 'Salvation to our God and the Lamb forever and ever. To him that loved us and washed us in his blood, and hath made us kings and priests to God his Father, to him be dominion and glory forever and ever.'[1]

And where they are, their brethren on the earth will ere long be. Is it not meet that we should endure with patience and fortitude on earth, since such rest and enjoyment are prepared for us in heaven? The phrase, brotherhood on earth, naturally leads the mind to the brotherhood in heaven. There is to be the permanent abode of the whole brotherhood. 'The gathering together' at the coming of the Lord, is to be there. 'Faithful is he who promised, who also will do it:' 'In my Father's house are many mansions,' accommodation for all the brotherhood; 'if it had not been so, I would have told you. I go to prepare a place for you; and if I go away, I will come again, and take you to myself, that where I am there ye may be also.' He became perfect through the accomplishment of his sufferings; and so, in a sense suited to our case, must we become perfect through the accomplishment of our sufferings. At the very utmost, we

[1] *Isa.* 38:14, *Rev.* 1:5, 6.

are not to be long in the world where our afflictions are to be accomplished, finished; we are to be forever in the better world, where the glorious results which infinite wisdom and kindness have wrought out by these afflictions, will continue unfolding themselves to our growing astonishment and delight throughout eternity.

Thus are all these afflictions accomplished here. The brotherhood who have passed the Jordan of death, and entered into the heavenly Canaan, are forever secure from the attacks of the wild beasts that roam the desert through which we are passing, and from all the afflictions which flow from these attacks. The old serpent shall never find his way into the restored paradise; and thither all the brotherhood are tending. Yet a little while and they shall all be there, safe and happy together, in their Father's house forever. This is surely great encouragement, abundant consolation.

2. The faithful promise

Let us now turn our attention to the still more explicit encouragement suggested by the faithful promise contained in the tenth verse; for, on careful inspection, it will be found to be a promise. The tenth verse is very generally considered as a prayer on the part of the apostle, that Christians might, amid their struggles and sufferings, be 'made perfect, stablished, strengthened, settled.' There can be no doubt that was his wish and prayer for them: but a closer consideration of the words convinces me, that this verse is not a prayer but a promise—not a request that God would confer certain most valuable and appropriate blessings on tempted, struggling, afflicted Christians, but a declaration that he will bestow them.

I think most careful readers of the Bible must have felt disappointed, that after so very graphic a view had been given of the dangers and struggles of the Christian, all that should have been said for his encouragement and comfort is, 'the same afflictions are fulfilled in your brethren that are in the world.' The rendering given by our translators of the tenth verse, is not literal—indeed from the text from which they translated, no strictly literal intelligible version could have been given. By the slightest of all changes, the putting one vowel in the place of another,[1] a change which the inquiries of critics have found not only to be authorized but required, the original passage is freed from all difficulty, and the encouragement administered to the tempted, struggling, afflicted believer, is as abundant and complete as we could expect or desire; indeed, 'above all that we could ask or think.' Literally rendered, the words thus amended, are, 'but the God of all grace, who hath called us,' or 'you, unto his eternal glory[2] by or in Christ Jesus, after ye have suffered a while, shall make you perfect,

[1] ε instead of α
[2] ἐν Χριστῷ Ἰησου.

strengthen, stablish, settle you.' It is as if he had said, such afflictions rising out of the attacks of the wicked one, must be endured by you; for they are the result of Divine appointment, an appointment reaching to and fulfilled in all your brotherhood in the world; but be not discouraged: 'The God of all grace, who has called you unto his eternal glory by Christ Jesus, after ye have suffered a while, shall make you perfect, stablish, strengthen, settle you.' The Christian, watching against the wiles, struggling against the assaults of the lion of hell, and suffering under the effects of his attacks, and their resistance, has need of abundant support, and encouragement, and consolation, and assuredly he has got it here.

There is strong consolation in the promise itself. 'God shall make you perfect, stablish, strengthen, settle you,' notwithstanding, nay, by means of these very afflictions. And then, what superadded encouragement and comfort is there in the adjuncts of the promise, in the manner in which the promise is given. For who promises? 'The God of all grace.' 'The God who has called you.' 'The God who has called you unto his eternal glory in Christ Jesus.' 'The God who has called you to this glory after ye have suffered a while.' Is there not in every one of these considerations a new and most exuberant fountain of spiritual encouragement and joy opened to the christian warrior, from which he may draw most refreshing draughts when fatigued by his conflicts with his great adversary, 'faint yet pursuing?' Well may he, like the Captain of his salvation, drink of the brook in the way, and lift up the head for renewed conflict, or untiring pursuit. Let us first, then, look at the matter of the promise, and then at the manner in which it is given.

(i.) The encouragement contained in the *promise itself*

Let us look at the promise, 'God shall make you perfect, stablish, strengthen, settle you.' The general meaning of the promise obviously is, God shall, notwithstanding, and even by means of these afflictions, promote your spiritual improvement, and add to your real happiness. All the figurative expressions are well fitted, and, with the exception of one of them,[1] frequently employed in the New Testament, to denote spiritual improvement and growth in holiness and comfort; and it has been supposed by many interpreters, that it is to no purpose to look for any specific meaning in each of these terms. They consider the promise as just a declaration, that through the preaching of God's word, the influence of his Spirit, and the overruling power of his providence, these afflictions should work together for their good, in the most extensive sense of the word, for making them really and, in the end, completely holy and happy, in entire conformity to the holy, holy, holy, ever-blessed

---

[1] σθενώσει is one of the ἅπαξ λεγομενα (*hapax legomena* Lit. 'once said'). A word which occurs only once in the New Testament.

53

One. We are disposed to think, however, that the apostle seldom heaps up words merely for the sake of emphasis, and that, in the passage before us, every one of the figurative expressions presents us with a distinct phase, as it were, of the blessings which God bestows on his people, under the afflictions, and by means of the afflictions which are connected with the assaults of the great adversary on them, and their resistance to these assaults.

It has been ingeniously supposed, that there is but one image in the whole passage, and that the different figurative expressions are connected representations of its different parts. Christians are supposed here, as in many places in the New Testament, to be represented as 'God's building,' 'a holy temple,'[1] and the whole of their christian improvement is termed their 'edification,' or building up. They are 'settled,' or the foundation is laid; then they are 'strengthened,' strong beams are fixed, and massy pillars raised; then they are 'stablished,' the building is roofed and protected from the injuries of the weather; and, finally, they are 'perfected.' Everything within and without is so fashioned, as to become a meet habitation for God through the Spirit. There is ingenuity enough here; but it is plain, if that had been the apostle's figure, the order of the expression would have been reversed. The four expressions seem, plainly, to bring

[1] *1 Cor.* 3:9, *Eph.* 2:21, 22, *1 Pet.* 2:5.

54

four distinct and unconnected figurative representations before the mind. Let us endeavour to ascertain their precise meaning.

(a.) *They shall be made perfect*

God promises, first, that he will 'make' Christians struggling with their great adversary 'perfect.' The word translated make perfect, properly signifies to make fully ready, to put in full order, to complete. It is used of fitting nets by mending them for being employed, and of the wickedness of the wicked fitting them as vessels of wrath for being destroyed. This is its meaning, when the apostle prays the God of peace, who brought again from the dead our Lord Jesus, that great Shepherd of the sheep, by the blood of the everlasting covenant, to make Christians 'perfect in every good work to do his will;'[1] that is, to fit them, by supplying what was wanting in them, for doing God's will in the performance of every good work; and when the Messiah, our High Priest, who must have somewhat to offer, is introduced as saying, 'a body hast thou prepared (the same word as here) me,' made ready for, fitted for me; and when the worlds are said to be 'framed (the same word) by the word of God,' prepared, fitted, for the purpose they were meant to serve.[2] In the passage before us, viewed as a promise to those who were

[1] *Heb.* 13:21.
[2] *Heb.* 10:5; 11:3.

called to conflict with an adversary, with whom in themselves they were very ill able to cope (and such general words must almost always be modified in their meaning, and limited in their reference by the context), its meaning plainly is, God will, by supplying all your defects, fit you for the conflict to which you are called. He will by his word and Spirit qualify you for all that you shall be called on to do and suffer in the combat. His grace shall be sufficient for you. He does not send you unarmed to the field of combat. He gives you the whole armour of God,[1] 'that ye may be able to stand against the wiles of the devil.' He gives you the girdle of truth, the breastplate of righteousness, the sandals of the preparation of the gospel of peace, the helmet of salvation, and the sword of the Spirit, which is the word of God; and he not only lays them down before you, but by his Spirit he enables you to put them on, and teaches you so to prove the various parts of this celestial panoply, as that in the day of battle you may turn them to good account in the combat with the alien and his armies. He will give you all the wisdom, all the courage, all the energy, that is necessary for successful conflict. This promise seems addressed to the Christian looking forward to the combat. The succeeding ones seem to refer to him when engaged in it.

[1] *Eph.* 6:13-18.

(b.) *They shall be established*

The second promise is, that God will 'stablish' them. To stablish is to keep firm and steadfast. The Christian is afraid that he shall fall before his enemies, that he shall not be able to keep his ground, that he shall lose courage, that he shall be turned back, with shame to himself and disgrace to his Lord and his cause, that he shall prove an apostate, that he shall not be able to hold fast the faith and its profession, that he shall find it difficult to stand, far more to withstand, that he shall make shipwreck of faith and a good conscience, and, instead of being crowned as a victor, shall be put to shame as a recreant[1] and castaway; but God meets these not unnatural apprehensions with the promise—I will stablish thee, I will keep thee from falling. The promise in the Second Epistle to the Thessalonians, 3:3, seems quite parallel with this: 'The Lord is faithful who shall stablish you, and preserve you from evil,' rather from the evil one.[2] It is just the evangelical version of the Old Testament oracle: 'Fear thou not; for I am with thee: be not dismayed; I am thy God: I will help thee; yea, I will uphold thee with the right hand of my righteousness.' He will 'put his law into their hearts;' and then, notwithstanding all the attempts of their spiritual enemies, 'they shall not depart from him.'[3]

---

[1] Coward, traitor.

[2] τοῦ πονηροῦ.

[3] *Isa.* 41:10, *Jer.* 32:40.

(c.) *They shall be strengthened*

The third promise is, God will 'strengthen' you. In the day of spiritual conflict he will enable them not only to stand, but to withstand; not only to keep their ground, but to press forward; not merely to defend themselves, but to attack their enemies. 'Out of weakness they shall' so 'wax strong,' as to 'turn to flight the armies of the aliens.' He will, by the effectual operation of his Spirit, through the instrumentality of his word, render the very efforts of their enemies to subdue them, the means of calling forth into action a power of which they themselves were before unconscious, so as to compel them to say, with a new feeling of the depth of truth contained in the words, 'When I am weak, then I am strong.' Thus does 'he give power to the faint, and to them who have no might he increaseth strength;' so that, though 'even the youths faint and be weary, and the young men utterly fail,' they, 'waiting on the Lord, renew their strength; they mount up on wings as eagles; they run, and are not weary; they walk, and are not faint.'[1] Thus it is, that amid the infirmities of his people, 'the power of Christ rests on them.' They are made 'strong in the Lord and in the power of his might;' and they 'go in the strength of the Lord God, making mention of his righteousness, even of his only.' 'In the Lord, in whom they have righteousness, they also have strength.'

[1] *Isa.* 40:29-31.

58

(d.) *They shall be settled*

The fourth and last promise is, 'God will settle you.' The word rendered 'settle' is equivalent to make to rest securely, as a building on its foundations. The idea is, the design of these attacks of Satan is to drive you from the foundation, Jesus, and the truth as it is in Jesus; but God will render all these attempts ineffectual by his preparing you for them, stablishing you, and strengthening you under them, and, by enabling you to stand and withstand, he will make them the means of fixing you firmer on that foundation than ever. Such afflictions, instead of producing apostasy, produce perseverance. 'We glory in tribulation,' that is, suffering in the cause of Christ, produced by the influence of the adversary, 'knowing that tribulation worketh patience,' that is, perseverance, increased attachment to the Saviour and his cause. Satan desires to have Christians that he may sift them, and scatter them to the winds of heaven; but through the grace of the Father, and the prayers of the Son, their faith fails not, and to their own increased comfort and confirmed hope, by this very sifting, they are proved to be, not chaff, but the Lord's wheat, which is to be 'gathered into his garner, while the chaff is burned with fire unquench- able.' These afflictions both prove the soundness of the foundation, leading the Christian more narrowly to examine it, and prove, too, that he is really built on the foundation. The Christian who is enabled to triumph over temptation, is stronger than if he had never been tempted; and there is no such firm believer as he who has battled with and fairly overcome, through him who loves him, all the doubts which the father of lies, and that most skilful sophister, the evil heart of unbelief under his influence, can suggest to the mind. This is the great object of God to settle his people on the foundation, the rock, Christ. 'This,' to borrow some of the beautiful thoughts of Leighton, 'is the only thing that perfects and strengthens us.' There is a wretched natural independency in us. We are apt to rest on something in ourselves. When we do so, we build castles in the air, imagining buildings without a foundation. A battle with our spiritual enemies will show us there is no safe footing there. If we do not seek firmer ground, we shall assuredly fall. Never shall we find safety, heart-peace, and progress in holiness, till we are driven from everything in ourselves, to make him all our strength, 'our rock, our fortress, our buckler, the horn of our salvation, and our high tower,' to do nothing, to attempt nothing, to hope for nothing, but in him. Then shall we find his fullness and all-sufficiency, and be 'more than conquerors through him who hath loved us.' Few things in Christian experience are more employed by God to bring his people into this state of settledness on the rock of Christ, than the afflictions rising out of the assaults of the evil one, and that resistance to these assaults, which are accomplished in the whole Christian brotherhood in the world. Thus can God bring good out of evil; strengthen faith by what was meant to overthrow it; increase the holiness and comfort of his people by what was meant to involve them in guilt, and depravity, and misery; make the wrath of devils, as well as men, to praise him, while he restrains the remainder thereof. 'He shall deliver them out of the mouth of the lion;' ay, 'he shall deliver them from every evil work,' every mischievous device, every malignant attempt of their adversary or his agents, earthly or infernal, and 'preserve them unto his heavenly kingdom.'

Such appears to be the import of the promise; such seems to be the perfecting, stablishing, strengthening, settling, of which the apostle speaks. To use the words of the pious and learned Bengel, 'He shall perfect (that no defect may remain in you), he shall stablish (that ye may be guilty of no backsliding), he shall strengthen (that ye may overcome every adverse power), and thus he shall settle you:' establish you more firmly than ever on the foundation, by those very means which were intended to remove you from it, and to convert into an unsightly heap of ruins, all the holy dispositions, and all the glorious hopes, which, like a stately edifice, 'polished after the similitude of a palace,' rested on that foundation.

(e.) *He who does all this for them is God*

This perfecting, and stablishing, and strengthening, and settling, are just what the Christian needs when called to combat, 'not with flesh and blood, but with the rulers of the darkness of this world, with spiritual wickedness in high places,' and the assurance of obtaining it is well fitted to encourage and comfort him. But to realise this encouragement and consolation, he must 'know and be sure' who it is that hath promised thus to perfect, and stablish, and strengthen, and settle. Such a promise from the most accomplished of men, from the highest of angels, from all good men and all good angels together, would sound like bitter mockery; but it is God who, by the mouth of his holy apostle, declares that he will perfect and stablish, strengthen and settle, the Christian combating with his subtle, active, cruel, and powerful spiritual adversary; and deeply as he feels how much is wanting in him for the conflict; how ready, how sure, if left to himself, to turn back in the day of battle; how powerless he is in the grasp of the strong man, the terrible one; how much in danger, so far as depends on anything in himself, of being permanently moved from his steadfastness, and torn from that rock of salvation on which the whole fabric of his holiness, and spiritual enjoyment, and hopes rest: this is enough to sustain and encourage him.

He can do all that he has here promised. He is infinite in power; and infinite, too, in wisdom. No enemy so powerful but he can restrain and subdue him; no enemy so crafty, but he can circumvent and disappoint him. No Christian so weak, but he can make him strong; no Christian so foolish, but he can make him wise. Is anything too hard for the Lord? To the Christian struggling with his spiritual foes, with a heart failing for fear, and an arm falling down with weariness, is addressed the words of the prophet: 'Why sayest thou, O Jacob, and speakest, O Israel, My way is hid from the Lord, and my judgment is passed over from my God? Hast thou not known, hast thou not heard, that the everlasting God, the Lord, the Creator of the ends of the earth, fainteth not, neither is weary? there is no searching of his understanding.'[1] There is no situation in which, in resisting your adversary, you can be placed, however full of painful exertion, anxiety, and suffering, in which he cannot give support, from which he cannot give deliverance.

Then he is disposed to do all that he has promised. He is 'rich in mercy;' he is 'ready to forgive.' The love that dictated the promise secures the accomplishment. 'If ye, being evil, know how to give good gifts to your children, how much more shall your Father in heaven,' who is not evil, who is good, only good, good continually, infinitely benignant, whose nature, as well as name, is love, how much more shall he 'give

[1] *Isa.* 40:27, 28.

good gifts to his children' when they ask them? But this truth, so richly fraught with encouragement, will come more fully before us when we come to speak of the adjuncts of the promise, or of the manner in which it is given.

Finally, here, he who gives the promise will most assuredly perform it. He can do it; for he is infinitely powerful and wise: he is disposed to do it; for he is infinitely kind and compassionate: he will do it; for he is inviolably faithful. He can do all things, but he cannot lie. Nothing is impossible with him but the denying himself. 'He is not a man that he should lie, nor the son of man that he should repent: hath he said it, and shall he not do it? hath he promised it, and shall he not make it good?' No, 'heaven and earth may pass away;' we know they shall pass away; 'but one iota, one tittle,' of his declarations 'shall not pass till all be fulfilled.'[1] As certainly as God is powerful and wise, merciful and faithful, so certain is it that he will not abandon the Christian resisting the subtle, active, powerful, cruel adversary of his soul; but will 'make him perfect, stablish, strengthen, settle' him, by the very means which were intended for his spiritual ruin, thus 'disappointing the devices of the crafty one, taking the wise in his own cunning, and turning the counsel of the froward headlong,'[2] saving the poor from the mouth of the devourer, and

[1] *Num.* 23:19, *Matt.* 5:18.
[2] *Job* 5:12.

rescuing them out of the hand of him who is mightier than they.[1]

Such is the promise; and is it not full of encouragement to the Christian amid the privations, and exertions, and sufferings, to which the resistance of his great adversary may expose him? Is it not well fitted to fill his heart with that joy of the Lord which is the strength of his people; to make him thank God, and take courage, saying, 'If God be with me, who can be against me? Rejoice not against me, O mine enemy: though I fall, I shall arise; though I sit in darkness, the Lord shall be a light to me. Greater is he who is with me than all that can be against me. Greater is He that is in us than he who is in the world.'[2]

(ii.) The encouragement contained in the *adjuncts* of the promise

But even this is not all the encouragement and comfort which this passage is fitted to administer to the struggling Christian warrior. The adjuncts of the promise have the same character with the promise itself; its manner as well as its matter is full of con-

---

[1] There is much emphasis given to the promise, by the insertion of the pronoun αὐτὸς between the nominative ὁ δὲ Θεὸς πάσης χάριτος and the verbs belonging to it, though it is not noticed in our version. It was just a thing for Bengel to notice. 'Αὐτὸς, *ipse—vos tantum vigilate et resistite hosti: reliqua Deus praestabit*.'—Conf. [confer or compare] אַךְ *Josh.* 13:6: conf. 1, *ej. cap.* [compare verse 1 of the same chapter] Translation: God himself—you have only to be watchful and resist your enemy—God, I say, will provide all the rest.

[2] *Rom.* 8:31, *Mic.* 7:8, 1 *John* 4:4.

solation. This is the next subject which calls for our consideration. What encouragement to him who resists the adversary to reflect, that he who has given to him such 'exceeding great and precious promises,' is 'the God of all grace,' the God 'who has called him,' 'called him to his eternal glory in or by Christ Jesus,' called him to this glory 'after he has suffered a while!' These are fruitful themes, respecting which our meditation should be profitable as well as sweet, on which 'our hearts should indite a good matter, and our tongues be as the pen of a ready writer.'[1]

(a.) *The God who has promised this is 'the God of all grace'*

The first consolatory and encouraging consideration here brought forward is, that the God who has promised these blessings is the 'God of all grace.' The proper signification of grace is kindness, the disposition to communicate happiness; but the term is also often employed to denote those actions or gifts in which this disposition is manifested. In both of these closely related significations of the word, God is the 'God of all grace.'

He is the all-gracious God. His name is 'the Lord; the Lord God, merciful and gracious, long-suffering, and abundant in goodness and truth.' His nature as well as his name is love. 'Fury,' malignity, passion, 'is not in him;' and, from the benignity of his nature, he

[1] *Psa.* 45:1.

is 'keeping mercy for thousands, forgiving iniquity, transgression, and sin.' 'This is his name, and this is his memorial to all generations.' From his perfect holiness he cannot but hate sin, and punish the sinner 'who goes on in his trespasses:' but he has 'no pleasure in the death of the wicked ;' on the contrary, He 'wills him to turn from his evil ways, that he may live,' be saved; while he is 'ready to forgive,' and 'delights in mercy,' in reference to those who, by the faith of the truth, are 'in Christ Jesus.' Every obstacle which prevents the manifestation of his love to them is removed. 'As a father pities his children, he pities them.' 'A woman may forget her sucking-child, she may not have compassion on the son of her womb;' but he never can forget them; and he can never remember them but with loving-kindness and tender mercy. And he rests in his love to them. He is 'Jehovah, who changes not;' 'the same yesterday, to-day, and forever.' 'The mountains may depart, the hills may be removed; but God's loving-kindness shall not depart from them, neither shall the covenant of his peace be removed by the Lord God, who has mercy on them.'

Is this his character? Then assuredly, amid all their afflictions, his children, 'the brotherhood,' may have 'abundant consolation and good hope.' If he has the power—and who can doubt that?—he must sustain, and comfort, and deliver. He can never allow them to become the prey of his and their adversary, who, 'like a roaring lion, goeth about, seeking whom he may devour.' 'He cannot deny himself;' and, if he cannot do this, he cannot but 'deliver them out of the mouth of this lion;' he cannot but deliver them 'from every evil work, and preserve them to his heavenly kingdom.'[1] Being 'the all-gracious God,' he will assuredly 'make them perfect, stablish, and strengthen them.'

God is also the God of all grace, in the sense of benefit. He is the author and bestower of all true happiness. When he is termed 'the God of all consolation,' the meaning is, all true comfort comes from him, and he bestows on his people abundance of all they need. When he is termed 'the God of peace,' the meaning is, that he is the author and bestower of true peace. So, when he is called 'the God of all grace,' the meaning may be, all blessings come from him; He is their ever-full, ever-flowing fountain, and to his people he communicates them, in all the variety and abundance that their wants can require, or their capacities receive. He 'blesses them with all spiritual and heavenly blessings.' What can he want, all whose need the God of grace, of all grace, promises to supply, 'according to his glorious riches'? He can, he will, fit for the combat; he can, he will, sustain during the conflict; he can, he will, make victorious in the conflict; he can, he will, reward after the conflict.

[1] *Exod.* 34:6, 7, *Ezek.* 18:23, 32, *Isa.* 54:10, 2 *Tim.* 4:18.

If there be any necessary blessing not included in 'all grace,' then the struggling Christian might have some cause to despond; but when Jehovah, 'God Almighty' (rather all-sufficient), says, I am 'the God of all grace,' and 'my grace is sufficient for thee;' well may he 'glory in tribulation,' 'count it all joy to be brought into manifold temptations,' and sing with the apostle, 'I have all, and abound; having nothing, I possess all things; I am complete in him. Most gladly will I glory in my infirmities, that the power of the God of all grace may rest on me; though troubled on every side, I am not distressed; though perplexed, I am not in despair; though persecuted, I am not forsaken; though cast down, I am not destroyed.'[1] The God of all grace has pledged his word and oath to me that I shall want no good thing; and what would I have, what could I have more?

(b.) *This God of all grace has 'called' the Christian 'in Christ Jesus'*

A second consoling and encouraging consideration is, this God of all grace has called the Christian in Christ Jesus. The 'called' is one of the distinguishing denominations of true Christians; in its fuller form 'the called of Christ Jesus;' 'the called according to God's purpose and grace;' 'the called who obtain the promised eternal inheritance;' and their calling is designated 'a high calling,' 'a holy calling,' a 'calling not according to

[1] *2 Cor.* 1:8, *Eph.* 1:8, *Phil.* 4:19, *Gen.* 17:1, *2 Cor.* 12:9, *2 Cor.* 4:8, 9.

works, but according to God's own purpose and grace, given us in Christ Jesus before the world began.' All mankind are called to God's service; and all mankind, to whom revelation comes, are 'called' by God to the enjoyment of his favour, as well as to obedience to his will; but in the case of the great majority, they are 'called' in vain, ineffectually called. They will not listen to the call; they very imperfectly understand it; they obstinately refuse to obey it. And were it not that the sovereign kindness of God accompanies, in certain cases, the call of providence and revelation, with the effectual operation of his Spirit, the outward call with the inward call, this would be universally the case with mankind. All would continue in a state of ignorance, unbelief, disobedience, and alienation from God. All men would always be what all by nature are, 'without God in the world.'

But in the case of 'a multitude that no man can number,' God, in the exercise of his sovereign mercy, accompanies the call of his word and providence with the special influence of his Spirit; so that the calling is not in vain, but effectual. 'It comes not in word merely, but in power, with the Holy Ghost, and much assurance.' The sinner hears the call of the God of all grace; he understands it, he believes it, he is sweetly constrained to comply with it. This calling is the same thing which the apostle styles 'election according to the foreknowledge and purpose of God,' by which Christians are spiritually separated from the rest of mankind, and put in possession of the blessings which flow from the shedding of the blood of sprinkling, which 'speaketh better things than that of Abel.' This 'effectual calling,' which is one of the characteristic blessings of the Christian salvation, and is the gate by which we enter into the enjoyment of all the rest, is well described in our Shorter Catechism as 'a work of God's Spirit, whereby, convincing us of our sin and misery, enlightening our minds in the knowledge of Christ, and renewing our wills, he doth persuade and enable us to embrace Jesus Christ, as he is freely offered to us in the gospel.' 'This is a call,' as Leighton beautifully says, 'that goes deeper than the ear, a word spoken home to within, a touch of the Spirit of God on the heart, which hath a magnetic power to draw it, so that it cannot choose but follow; and yet freely and sweetly chooses to follow; doth most gladly open to let in Jesus Christ, and his sweet government, upon his own terms; takes him, and all the reproaches and troubles that can come with him; and well it may, seeing, beyond a little passing trouble, abiding eternal glory.'

This calling is said to be 'in Christ Jesus,' that is, either 'persons standing in a peculiar relation to Christ Jesus, identified as it were with him, are its subjects;' or, 'through Christ Jesus,' through his mediation, in consequence of his atonement, by his Spirit and Word. It is probably the last of these that is here the apostle's idea. Men are called by the Father, through the Son. The fundamental blessing was enjoyed by those to whom the apostle wrote. The God of all grace had called them out of darkness into his marvellous light; out of subjection to sin, and the world, and the god of this world, into the glorious liberty of his children. The communication of this blessing is a proof that God loves with a special love the individual on whom it is conferred; and a distinct intimation, that all the other blessings of that salvation, of which this is a constituent part, shall in due time be bestowed. The fact of their being called by the God of all grace, involves in it satisfactory evidence, that their spiritual adversary shall not ultimately prevail against them, that their afflictions cannot be permanent, and that they shall be made conducive to their final salvation. Listen to the Apostle Paul's development of this argument. 'We know that all things' — he is referring to the afflictions which are accomplished in the brotherhood in this world — 'We know that all things work together for good to them that love God; who are the called according to his purpose. For whom he did foreknow, he also did predestinate to be conformed to the image of his Son, that he might be the first-born among many brethren. Moreover, whom he did predestinate, them he also called; and whom he called, them he also justified; and whom he justified, them he also glorified. What shall we say to these things? If God be for us, who can be against us?'[1] Can the wiles or the ferocity of the roaring lion, the fraud or the fury of the great adversary, accomplish our ruin, who are the called, the called of the God of all grace?

(c.) *The God of all grace has called Christians to his eternal glory*

A third consolatory and encouraging consideration is, that 'the God of all grace has called the Christian to his eternal glory.' The phrase, 'called unto God's eternal glory,' may either signify, called in order eternally to promote the glory of God, or called to enjoy or participate in the eternal glory of God. In either case, the words express a truth, and a truth well fitted to comfort and encourage Christians while struggling with their spiritual enemies.

The calling of the Christian, and the conferring on him all the blessings of the christian salvation which grow out of it, have for their ultimate object, like everything else in the new creation as in the old, the manifestation of God, the illustration of his excellence, the display of his glory. This idea is very finely brought out by the apostle, in the first chapter of his Epistle to the Ephesians: 'The God and Father of our Lord Jesus Christ hath blessed us with all heavenly and spiritual blessings in Christ; according as he hath chosen us in him before the foundation of the world, that we should be holy and without blame before him

[1] *Rom.* 8:28-31.

in love: having predestinated us unto the adoption of children by Jesus Christ to himself, according to the good pleasure of his will, *to the praise of the glory of his grace*, wherein he hath made us accepted in the Beloved: in whom we have redemption through his blood, the forgiveness of sins, according to the riches of his grace; wherein he hath abounded towards us in all wisdom and prudence; having made known unto us the mystery of his will, according to his good pleasure, which he hath purposed in himself: that, in the dispensation of the fullness of the times, he might gather together into one all things in Christ, both which are in heaven, and which are on earth, even in him: in whom also we have obtained an inheritance, being predestinated according to the purpose of him who worketh all things according to the counsel of his will; that we should be *to the praise of his glory*, who first trusted in Christ. In whom ye also trusted,' or rather have received an inheritance, 'after that ye heard the word of truth, the gospel of your salvation: in whom also, after that ye believed, ye were sealed with that Holy Spirit of promise, which is the earnest of our inheritance,' both ours and yours, 'until the redemption of the purchased possession, *unto the praise of his glory*.'[1] Were the Christian to be allowed to fall a prey to his spiritual enemies, his calling, instead of being to God's eternal glory, would give

[1] *Eph.* 1:3-14.

cause to the adversary to speak reproachfully, saying, 'the Lord was not able to bring them into the land which he had promised them.' But Jehovah is determined, even through the means of those babes and sucklings whom he calls, to perfect praise to himself, and to 'still the enemy and the avenger.' He has called them to be his people, and 'formed them for himself, and they shall show forth his praise.' His power, and wisdom, and faithfulness, and kindness, shall be illustriously displayed in the salvation of all the called ones. 'His counsel shall stand, and he will do all his pleasure.'[1] This is truth, important truth; truth naturally enough expressed by the words, and truth well-fitted to encourage and strengthen the Christian when conflicting with his great adversary.

Yet we are inclined to think the other view of the words expresses the apostle's thought. He has called them to a participation of his eternal glory. The glory of God sometimes signifies the approbation of God. Thus the Jews are said to 'receive honour (the same word) one of another, and not to seek the honour that cometh from God only.' Thus, all are said to 'have sinned and come short of the glory of God;' and believers, justified through believing, are represented as 'exulting in the hope of that glory,' that approbation, of which they had come short, and in which true glory and happiness consist. Here, as in some

---

[1] *Num.* 14:16, *Psa.* 8:2, *Isa.* 43:21; 46:10.

other places, there can be little doubt that 'the glory of God' is the celestial blessedness; but still it is the celestial blessedness in a particular aspect. The glory of God is that which makes God glorious; his eternal glory that which makes him eternally glorious. Now, what is it that makes God glorious? His own inherent excellences, especially his moral excellences, his righteousness and benignity; in one word, his holiness. He is 'glorious in holiness.' Now, the grand ultimate object of the calling of the Christian is, that he, to the highest degree of which his nature is capable, may be made a partaker of God's holiness, which is his glory. He is called to the fellowship, as well as predestinated to be conformed to the image of God's dear Son, who is the 'brightness of his glory and the express image of his person.' It is the purpose of God in calling him, and in giving him the adoption of sons to which he has been predestinated, that he shall be holy, as he, the holy, holy, holy One, is holy, perfect as he is perfect. It is his purpose that, in the kingdom of their Father, the Father of Lights, his called ones shall shine forth radiant with his light, glorious in his glory; and in the only sense in which eternity can be truly predicted of them, or of anything that belongs to them, that their glory shall be eternal, that 'they shall shine as the brightness of the firmament, and like stars in the firmament, forever and ever.' Now, no assault from Satan, no calamities, no afflictions, can prevent this glorious consummation—nay, all

their afflictions will be found to have been but disciplinary means of preparing them for this grand result
of all the Divine dispensations to them—the making
them 'partakers of his holiness,' which is his glory.[1]

(d.) *The afflictions are moderate in degree, short in duration, and form a part of the Divine plan for their ultimate
salvation*

A fourth consolatory and encouraging consideration
suggested, is derived from the peculiar character of
the afflictions to which the brotherhood are exposed;
they are comparatively moderate in degree and short
in duration; they form a part of the Divine plan re-
sulting from Divine appointment; and they are closely
connected with the great end of their calling,—their
coming to a participation in the glory of God. The
God of all grace has called you to his eternal glory 'after ye have suffered a while,' or a little. These words,
'after ye have suffered a while,' have been closely
connected by some with the clause that follows,
'After ye have suffered a while, make you perfect,
stablish, strengthen, settle you.' The laws of the language would warrant either mode of connection; but
it is plain that the promise is not one which is to be
fulfilled till Christians have suffered a while. The first
promise refers to preparation for suffering, the two
next to help under suffering, the last to the happy
result of suffering. God calls his people to participate

[1] *1 Cor.* 1:9, *Rom.* 8:29, *Heb.* 12:10.

in his eternal glory, but not to participate in it 'till they have suffered a while,' or a little. The word may refer either to time or degree. In either case, a truth, and a consolatory one, is expressed. The afflictions to which the brotherhood are exposed in this world are comparatively moderate in degree. They are often heavy when compared with those of other men, and are often felt as heavy by those who bear them, making them breathe out, 'I am oppressed; undertake for me.' They are always lighter than they easily might be; always lighter than strict justice would require them to be. Everything to a sinner, short of the severest suffering he is capable of, is mercy. God does not, however, 'suffer them to be tempted above what they are able to bear, but with the temptation gives a way of escape, that they may be able to bear it;' and especially they are moderate when compared with the 'far more exceeding and eternal weight of glory' which is to follow them.

They are limited in duration. Seasons of very severe affliction are not ordinarily of long duration; they bear usually but a small proportion to the whole of human life. How inconceivably small a proportion do they bear to the eternity of coming glory! Surely, then, whether he look on their measure or their period, their degree or their duration, the Christian may well 'reckon the sufferings of the present time not worthy to be compared with the glory which shall be revealed in him.'

Then, these afflictions are a part of the Divine plan. It is as much a part of the Divine plan to put them in possession of the fellowship of his eternal glory after they have suffered a while, as to put them in possession of it at all. 'It is the Father's good pleasure to give them the kingdom;' but it is equally the Father's good pleasure that 'through much tribulation they enter into that kingdom.' It is his determination that they 'shall reign with Christ,' but it is equally his determination that they 'shall first suffer with him.'[1]

And finally, here, this connection, though an appointed one, is not an arbitrary one. The glory not only comes after the sufferings, but it is, in some sense, the result of them. Afflictions are, under the Divine blessing, appropriate means of sanctification; of forming the character which fits for the holy happiness of heaven; 'that prepared place for a prepared people.' The truth on this subject is strikingly stated by the apostle from his own experience: 'Though our outward man perish, yet the inward man is renewed day by day. For our light affliction, which is but for a moment, worketh for us a far more exceeding and eternal weight of glory; while we look not at the things which are seen, but at the things which are not seen: for the things which are seen are temporal; but the things which are unseen are eternal.'[2] 'Who would refuse to suffer a while, a little while, anything

[1] *Luke* 12:32, *Acts* 14:22, *Rom.* 8:17, 2 *Tim.* 2:12.
[2] 2 *Cor.* 4:16-18.

outward or inward he sees fit? How soon shall this be over, past, and overpaid in the very entry, the beginning of that glory, that shall never end!'[1]

[1] Leighton.

PART IV.

CONCLUSION

It now only remains that we shortly illustrate the concluding clause of the verse, which is very generally considered as a doxology. The words are, 'To him be glory and dominion forever and ever, Amen.' The word *be* is inserted by our translators, who consider the clause as an ascription of glory and dominion to God. The word *is* might as well have been inserted, in which case it is an assertion that glory and dominion belong to God. Had the preceding verse been a prayer or a thanksgiving, the words would likely have been meant as a doxology; but following a promise, they seem to state something corresponding to the promise. 'His is the glory forever and ever,' and, therefore, he can confer on his people that glory to which he has called them, after they have suffered a while. He has not only an essential glory peculiar to himself, and of which no creature can participate. He has a communicable glory; 'the riches of his glory,' as the apostle expresses it, by the bestowing of which on others he can make them glorious. He is 'the Father of glory,' as well as the God of all grace, who can give not only grace but also glory. And as 'glory forever and ever' belongs to him who has 'called Christians to his eternal glory after they have suffered a while;' so 'dominion' (a word denoting both power and authority) 'forever and ever' belongs to him, who, as the God of grace, promises that he will make perfect, stablish, strengthen, and settle his people. He has power and right to do whatever pleases him, and therefore can do what he has said. 'His is the greatness, and the power, and the glory, and the victory, and the majesty: for all in the heaven and in the earth is his; his is the kingdom, and he is exalted as head above all. Both riches and honor come of Him, and he reigneth over all; and in his hand is power and might; and in his hand it is to make great, and give strength to all.' He who has glory forever and ever, can give to his called that fellowship of his eternal glory which he has promised; and he whose is the dominion, the power, and the authority forever, is 'of power to establish his people according to the gospel and the preaching of Jesus Christ.' He is 'able to do exceeding abundantly above all that we can ask or think, according to the power that worketh in us.' 'He can make them perfect in every good work to do his will, working in them that which is well-pleasing in his sight.' He is 'able to keep them from falling, and to present them faultless before the presence of his glory with exceeding joy.'[1] It deserves notice that the apostle concludes his epistle as he began it, by turning the minds of those to whom he wrote to God, and to the same features in the Divine character—those which make him a fit object of our love and dependence—his kindness and his might. In the beginning he speaks of him as the God of abundant mercy, who has power to keep his people for the inheritance he has destined for them, and for which he is preparing them: and here he speaks of him as the God of all grace, whose is the dominion, to whom all the power and authority rightfully belong.

The apostle adds an emphatic 'Amen'—a word, in reference to statement, expressive of firm faith; in reference to promises, of confident hope and ardent desire. In the first instance it is equivalent to 'It is most certainly so; this is the very truth most sure.' In the second, 'I trust it shall be so; I desire that it may be so.' Such, then, is the comfort and encouragement by which the apostle seeks to strengthen the brotherhood amid the afflictions which must be accomplished in them in the world.

If anything extrinsic could add force to the sentiments expressed in these words—sentiments so instinct with life, so fitted to impart spiritual vigour to the exhausted spirit of the Christian, worn out with watching the wiles and resisting the attacks of his great

---

[1] *1 Chron.* 29:11, 12, *Rom.* 16:25, *Eph.* 3:20, *Heb.* 13:21, *Jude* 24.

adversary—it is to be found in the circumstances of him who uttered them. 'Truth,' such truth, 'from his lips prevails with double sway.' The word of warning, the word of instruction, the word of promise, the word of encouragement, come all with peculiar force from the lips of him to whom, on a most memorable occasion, the Master said, 'Simon, Simon, Satan hath desired to have you, that he may sift you as wheat, but I have prayed for thee that thy faith fail not; and when thou art converted, strengthen thy brethren.' He speaks the things which he knew, he testifies what he had seen and felt. He had disregarded the Master's warning, and the consequence had been shameful discomfiture in his conflict with the great enemy; aggravated sin, followed by deep penitence, and confirmed attachment to the cause of Christ. He had found how faithful he is who had promised, and how able he is to do as he had said. He had preserved him from apostasy when on its very brink; and, notwithstanding the partial success of his spiritual adversary, he had 'stablished, strengthened, settled' him; 'set him on a rock and established his goings.' How emphatic the warning, 'Your enemy, the devil, goeth about like a roaring lion, seeking whom he may devour,' from him who had experienced both his wiles and his ferocity, and would bear about with him the scars of his wounds while he lived! How forcible the injunction, 'Resist the devil;' and that you may do so, 'Be sober, and wakeful, and steadfast in the faith,' from him, who, notwithstanding repeated warnings, did not watch and pray, and therefore entered into temptation, and fell before it, and whose failure in faith had brought him so near destruction and despair; had made him fall into sin, and but for the God of all grace would have made him fall into perdition! How consoling and encouraging the promise, 'The God of all grace, who hath called you unto his eternal glory by Christ Jesus, will make you perfect, stablish, strengthen, settle you; His is the glory and the dominion forever and ever,' from him whom the God of all grace, in the person of his Son, had so 'out of weakness made strong,' so strengthened in the faith as to make him one of the chief pillars of the church while he lived; and when he died, enabled him to glorify God, confessing, amid the protracted tortures of a peculiarly cruel martyrdom, the Master whom once he had thrice denied! We cannot help thinking that the Saviour's words, 'When thou art converted, strengthen thy brethren,' were ringing in the apostle's ears when he wrote these words. And, certainly, never were addressed to the tempted, struggling, worn out, afflicted Christian soldier, words more full of warning, instruction, consolation, and encouragement. They have, by the accompanying power of the Spirit of Jesus, strengthened many a brother. They have been 'words in season' to many a tempted, afflicted, perplexed, downcast, weary heart; and will continue to be so, as long as these afflictions continue to be accomplished in the brotherhood in the world. Oh, may we, my brethren, through their means, be made humble and cautious, vigilant and believing, 'steadfast and immovable,' rooted and built up in Christ, 'strengthened with all might, according to his glorious power, unto all patience and long-suffering with joyfulness; giving thanks to the Father who hath made us meet to be partakers of the inheritance of the saints in light; who hath delivered us from the power of darkness, and hath translated us unto the kingdom of his dear Son;' so that, full of the strength which is the result of the joy of the Lord, glorying in tribulation, and rejoicing in hope of the glory of God, we may 'walk worthy of the Lord unto all pleasing, being fruitful in every good work, and increasing in the knowledge of God.'[1] 'Consider what has been said, and the Lord give you understanding in all things.'[2]

---

[1] *Col.* 1:10-13.
[2] 2 *Tim.* 2:7.

OTHER TITLES FROM

THE BANNER OF TRUTH TRUST

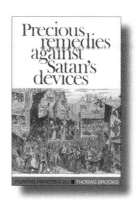

Precious Remedies against Satan's Devices
Thomas Brooks
Puritan Paperback series, 256pp.
ISBN: 978 0 85151 002 6

'Brooks displays a profound grasp of the subtlety of Satan, the widespread ramifications of sin and the depth of corruption of the human heart. He traces all the devious ways by which Satan approaches, and declares the remedies which God has provided in His Word and by His Spirit. This is a very readable book. It is full of lively illustrations and pithy sayings such as: 'He that will play with Satan's bait will quickly be taken with Satan's hook.'
Evangelical Times

'Brooks scatters stars with both his hands; he hath dust of gold; in his storehouse are all manner of precious stones.'
C. H. Spurgeon

Thomas Charles' Spiritual Counsels
Edited by Edward Morgan
Clothbound, 520pp.
ISBN: 978 0 85151 656 1

Thomas Charles (1755–1814) was a leader of the Calvinistic Methodists in North Wales. This volume comprises twenty-six essays which cover just over 200 pages and many extracts from his letters and papers.

'The book is worth reading for the essays alone, which cover a wide range of subjects. They are easy to read and they are full of application. The writer speaks from experience of knowing God in his daily life. The extracts from his letters are shorter in length than the essays, but are still interesting. Each letter has been given a subject title which will be of value to a minister or lay worker who wishes to use this as a reference book. The book also includes a biographical introduction written by Iain H. Murray.'

The Gospel Magazine